PRINCE EDWARD ISLAND
BOOK OF
Everything

Everything you wanted to know about
Prince Edward Island and were going
to ask anyway

Martha Walls

MACINTYRE PURCELL PUBLISHING INC.

TO OUR READERS

Every effort has been made by authors and editors to ensure that the information
enclosed in this book is accurate and up-to-date. We revise and update annually,
however, many things can change after a book gets published. If you discover any
out-of-date or incorrect information in the Prince Edward Island Book of Everything,
we would appreciate hearing from you via our website, www.bookofeverything.com.

Copyright 2017 MacIntyre Purcell Publishing Inc.

MacIntyre Purcell Publishing Inc.
194 Hospital Rd.
Lunenburg, Nova Scotia
B0J 2C0
(902) 640-3350

www.macintyrepurcell.com
info@macintyrepurcell.com

Printed and bound in Canada by Marquis.
Design and layout: Channel Communications and Alex Hickey

Cover photo: flickr.com
Photos: istockphoto: page 6, 16, 34, 42, 64, 76, 90, 182
123 RF: page 8, 48, 112, 136, 154, 172
Map courtesy of BBCanada.com

Library and Archives Canada Cataloguing in Publication
Walls, Martha, 1972-
Prince Edward Island Book of Everything / Martha
Walls.
ISBN 978-0-9738063-6-6
Prince Edward Island--Guidebooks. I. Title.
FC2607.W35 2007   971.1704'5
C2007-901781-9

Introduction

Of course no book can really be about everything, but we hope the *Prince Edward Island Book of Everything* comes close to capturing the essence of PEI. We could have filled volumes. In fact, our most difficult task was determining not what to write about, but what to exclude.

As an expat Islander, this book has been a homecoming for me. From the red sand beaches of an August evening, to fiery political debates, from the ubiquitous Anne of Green Gables, to Island slang, PEI is many things to the diverse people who call themselves 'Islanders.'

This book is a product of teamwork. A team of writers worked tirelessly, combing through material to bring together these facts and stories. Samantha Amara tackled many chapters with enthusiasm, insight and a keen editing pen. Lynn MacIntyre wrote many sections with her trademark promptness and accuracy. Carrie Anne MacIsaac has told us about one of Islanders' favourite topics – the weather. Julie Gilvear and Kelly Inglis expertly administered this project and Kelly read and edited the manuscript, offering valuable insight. We would also like to thank all those Islanders who shared with us their insight about their province. Islanders are, without a doubt, PEI's greatest attribute.

In the summer of 1959, a young clergyman and his family arrived to a new life on PEI. The beginning was inauspicious. Their home, undergoing repairs, was uninhabitable. And yet, the distressed trio immediately found a warm temporary home with none other than Walter Shaw, one day premier of PEI. My parents will never forget this hospitality, and they fell in love with their new home province. I can't thank them enough for giving our family Island roots. Whoever said you can't go home again was clearly not from PEI.

— Martha Walls, for everyone at the
PEI Book of Everything

Table of Contents

The Island Hymn

In the early spring of 1908, renowned writer Lucy Maud Montgomery penned *The Island Hymn* in homage to the Island home she loved. It was performed publicly for the first time soon after, to a melody composed specifically for the ballad by Lawrence W. Watson.

The Island Hymn

Fair Island of the sea
We raise our song to thee,
The bright and blest;
Loyally now we stand
As brothers, hand in hand,
And sing God save the land
We love the best.

Upon our princely Isle
May kindest fortune smile
In coming years;
Peace and prosperity
In all her borders be,
From every evil free,
And weakling fears.

Prince Edward Isle, to thee
Our hearts shall faithful be
Where'er we dwell;
Forever may we stand
As brothers, hand in hand,
And sing God save the land
We love so well.

Prince Edward Island

A Timeline

11,000 Before Present: Evidence suggests the first inhabitants take up residence in territory that would one day be Prince Edward Island.

5,000 Before Present: Ocean levels rise, ushering in PEI's future status as an island.

1534: Jacques Cartier is the first European to record a sighting of PEI and its Mi'kmaq inhabitants. He declares it "the fairest land that may possibly be seene."

1720: The Island's first continuous French settlement is founded at Port La Joie. Throughout the period of French occupation, the Island is called Ile Saint-Jean.

1758: Following the expulsion of Acadians in Nova Scotia in 1755, the British turned their attention to the Island. More than 3,000 settlers were deported, and more than 700 of those died in shipwrecks.

1762: Charlottetown is founded, named in honour of Charlotte, the wife of King George III. Three years later it is made the capital.

1763: The Island is annexed to British Nova Scotia and its name anglicized to St. John's Island.

1767: The Island is divided into 67 parcels of land and distributed by lottery to British nobles. When most landowners fail to meet the stipulation that their land be settled within ten years, British officials do nothing, raising the ire of settlers who, for next century, fight to be rid of absentee landlords.

1768: Lieutenant Governor Franklyn of Nova Scotia orders the Island's first census under British Rule.

1769: St. John's Island gets its own constitution and its government is moved from Nova Scotia to Charlottetown.

1787: The Island's first newspaper, *The Royal American Gazette and Weekly Intelligencer of the Island of Saint John*, is published in Charlottetown but folds after just a year.

1798: St. John's Island is re-named Prince Edward Island in honour of Prince Edward, Duke of Kent (1767-1820).

Did you know...

. . . that when the Acadian village of Havre St-Pierre (present day St. Peters Harbour) was uprooted in the deportation of 1758, local townspeople buried the bell of the parish church to guard it against British confiscation? In 1871, a farmer ploughing his fields discovered the bell, which now hangs in the Church of St. Alexis at Rollo Bay.

1803: The Earl of Selkirk arrives on the Island with 800 Scottish settlers, the largest single immigrant group to settle on the Island.

1834: Prince of Wales College, the Island's first institution of higher learning, is established in Charlottetown.

1864: Delegates from Canada East, Canada West and the Maritime colonies meet in Charlottetown to discuss possible Confederation.

Take 5 — CATHERINE CALLBECK'S FIVE MOST IMPORTANT EVENTS IN ISLAND POLITICS

Catherine Callbeck was the first woman to be elected as a premier in Canada. She is a former member of parliament and is currently a senator from Prince Edward Island. She has been an active businessperson and has had a long and active involvement with charitable and public service groups at all levels.

1. **Responsible Government** – This was achieved in 1851 and for the first time the Cabinet became accountable to the people through the Legislative Assembly.

2. **Confederation** – Prince Edward Island joined the rest of Canada in 1873 and, as Canada's smallest province, occupies a distinct position in the country.

3. **The Land Question** – After more than a century under the control of absentee landlords, Islanders finally achieved a settlement of this contentious issue following Confederation when it acquired the means to purchase the remaining landlord estates.

4. **Voting Rights for Women** – This was finally achieved by the 1923 provincial election, when for the first time, the other half of the population received the right to vote.

5. **The Confederation Bridge** – Following a referendum, the federal and provincial governments proceeded with the construction of a fixed link to the mainland.

1866: Fire devastates Charlottetown, razing two hundred buildings downtown.

1867: Concerned that its political and economic interests would be compromised, PEI opts not to join in Confederation with Ontario, Quebec, Nova Scotia and New Brunswick.

1871: Construction of the Prince Edward Island Railway begins.

1873: Lured by the promise of debt relief and slightly improved federal representation, PEI joins Confederation – the last province to do so until Newfoundland and Labrador's entry in 1949.

1874: Lucy Maude Montgomery, famed author of *Anne of Green Gables*, is born in Clifton, PEI.

1883: The *Marco Polo*, dubbed the fastest clipper ship in the world, runs aground 300 yards off the coast of Cavendish in a fierce July storm.

1908: *Anne of Green Gables* is first published.

1917: The Island's first permanent rail-car ferry, *The Prince Edward Island*, begins service between Borden and Cape Tormentine, NB.

1937: Prince Edward Island National Park, which encompasses the north Gulf of St. Lawrence shore, is designated.

1938: The car-rail ferry, *The Prince Edward Island*, is retrofitted with a vehicle deck to accommodate increasing automobile traffic.

1942: Lucy Maude Montgomery dies and is buried in Cavendish.

1943: Montgomery is declared a person of Canadian National Historic Significance.

1964: The Confederation Centre of the Arts is built to commemorate the 1864 Charlottetown Conference.

1965: The musical *Anne of Green Gables* opens at Confederation Centre. Still performed each year, it is Canada's longest running musical.

1969: The University of Prince Edward Island is incorporated by provincial legislation to create "a single, public, non-denominational institution of higher education."

1969: Holland College created by official proclamation to "provide a broadened range of educational opportunity particularly in the field of applied arts and technology."

1972: *Anne of Green Gables* finds life on the big screen with the release of the BBC's five-part mini-series of the same name. A second adaptation airs on CBC in 1985.

1983: Public Works Canada reviews a $640-million dollar proposal for a bridge to the Island.

1989: Rail service on the Island is discontinued.

1992: Islanders vote in a plebiscite on the construction of a fixed crossing to the Island. A majority 59.4 percent says 'yes' to the idea, while 40.6 percent say 'no.'

Did you know...

. . . that potatoes were produced on PEI as early as 1771? That year, the colony's governor reported a bumper crop.

1993: Construction on the Confederation Bridge begins. The mammoth undertaking costs $1 billion.

1993: Catherine Sophia Callbeck is elected premier of PEI, becoming the first female premier in Canada.

Take 5 — COWS TOP FIVE
COWS ICE CREAM FLAVOURS

COWS began to make ice cream in 1983 with an old-fashioned family recipe that originated in Cavendish. In a very short time the demand for COWS ice cream and products increased dramatically, and COWS quickly became a Prince Edward Island symbol as identifiable as Anne herself. Despite the growth that COWS has experienced, the same old-fashioned ingredients are still used today when making the 32+ flavours.

1. **Wowie Cowie:** This most popular COWS flavour contains vanilla ice cream, English toffee, chocolate flakes and Moo crunch, a Skor bar-like treat made in our Anne of Green Gables chocolate factory.

2. **Vanilla:** You just can't beat vanilla. COWS is made with real cream, eggs, sugar and pure vanilla which is slow-churned into a rich, creamy old-fashioned ice cream much like that which would have been enjoyed by the children of Avonlea at the time of Anne of Green Gables.

3. **Strawberry:** This delectable treat is made with our vanilla ice cream and fresh Island strawberries.

4. **Chocolate:** The secret to this flavour is its infusion with pure cocoa imported from Holland.

5. **Gooey Mooey:** This boasts vanilla ice cream, loaded with English toffee and caramel cups.

1997: On May 31st, at 5:15pm, the first vehicles cross the 12.9 km Confederation Bridge.

1998: Land on the western end of the Greenwich Peninsula is added to the Prince Edward Island National Park.

2003: The over-fished cod fishery on the southern Gulf of St. Lawrence is closed.

2005: A Wind Energy Institute is announced for Prince Edward Island. The first in Canada, the Institute supports the development of wind power generation.

2006: Agriculture, Fisheries and Aquaculture Minister Jim Bagnall and Tourism Minister Philip Brown announce the reopening of the recreational cod fishery.

2009: Prince Edward Island hosts the 2009 Canada Summer Games. Approximately 4,400 athletes, coaches, and managers are expected to arrive for the two-week period in August.

2015: The Prince Edward Island Liberal Party wins a third straight election under the leadership of Wade MacLauchlan, a former president of the University of Prince Edward Island. The Party took 18 of the 27 seats up for grabs.

2015: Wade MacLauchlan is the first member of the Order of Canada to become premier of a province. He is also the first openly gay premier of Prince Edward Island and the first openly gay man to be premier of a province.

PEI Essentials

Origin of the Name: Prior to the arrival of Europeans, the Mi'kmaq called their Island home Epekwitk, often translated to mean 'resting on the waves.' In the 18th century, the French established a small colony called Ile St. Jean, a name anglicized to St. John's Island when the British assumed control in 1763. In 1799, the Island got its current handle when British officials renamed it Prince Edward Island in honour of Edward, Duke of Kent, the father of Queen Victoria.

Official Nickname: The Gentle Island

Other Nicknames: The Garden Province, The Million Acre Farm, Spud Island or simply, The Island

Capital City: Charlottetown

Provincial Bird: The Blue Jay (*Cyanocitta cristata*). In 1997, more than twenty years after Islanders selected the bird in a plebiscite, the Blue Jay was officially designated the provincial bird. Like all true Islanders, the Blue Jay lives on the Island year round.

Provincial Flower: The Lady's Slipper (*Cypripedium acaule*). Designated the provincial flower in 1947, this orchid's petals form a pouch resembling a slipper.

Provincial Tree: The Red Oak (*quercus rubra*). Growing at a rate of two feet per year and reaching heights of 100 feet, this provincial tree was widely used by early settlers to make furniture and barrels.

Rin PRINCE EDWARD AUGUSTUS

On November 2nd, 1767, Prince Edward Augustus, the fourth son of King George III and his wife Charlotte, was born at Buckingham Palace, London. Although born with a royal spoon in his mouth, Edward's life would be a difficult one. As a youth, Edward and his father were estranged and King George did his best to keep his son out of England. Very unhappily, Edward received a military education in Europe where he amassed a sizeable debt that would plague him for the rest of his life.

Prince Edward excelled in military service and quickly rose in the ranks. By 1790, he was a colonel based in Gibraltar. Known for his draconian discipline, men who served under him complained of his harsh command. In 1791, Edward's regiment was relocated to Quebec where the young Prince became part of the colony's social elite. When war erupted between France and England in 1793, Edward, then a Major-General, was sent to Halifax, charged with commanding the forces of New Brunswick and Nova Scotia. Still exhibiting his penchant for iron- fisted command, he was exceedingly unpopular with the troops. Nevertheless, he did much for Halifax as it was under his watch that the city was revitalized and a new Citadel constructed.

In 1798, a fall from a horse left Prince Edward severely injured and he returned to his native London to recuperate. On his arrival home, the wayward royal was made Duke of Kent and Strathearn, promoted to General and then named Commander-in-Chief of the forces in British North America. His injured leg healed, and he

The Tartan: Designed by Jean Reid, the reddish brown of PEI's provincial tartan represents the red soil, the green its trees and the grass, the white the caps on the waves and the yellow the sun.

Coat of Arms: The 1905 Coat of Arms, granted by King Edward VII, features a shield and a gold Heraldic Lion stretched across the top, borrowed from the Coat of Arms of the Island's namesake, Prince Edward,

returned to Halifax in 1899. Ill-health, however, cut his stay short. A return dispatch to Gibraltar followed in 1802, but also ended quickly when he was recalled in a hailstorm of complaints about his extreme disciplinary tactics. Prince Edward's days of active military service were over.

When Edward returned home, the rift between he and the King had still not healed and without his father's favour Edward was unable to secure an important office. As a result, he spent his life in retirement at his London estate, serving a number of charities.

Meanwhile, Edward's love life became a matter of public scrutiny. For 27 years he had a relationship with commoner Thérèse-Bernardine Mongenet. By 1818, however, Edward had a difficult choice to make. Still beset by debt, he had been forced to relocate to Brussels. He was also facing intense pressure to marry and produce an heir, particularly after the 1817 death of his sister, Princess Charlotte, second in line to the throne.

Given his fiscal difficulties, marriage into a moneyed family was in order; Mongenet's family did not fit the bill. And so, in May 1818, Prince Edward married Victoria Mary Louisa, widow of the Prince of Leiningen. A year later, the couple gave birth to a daughter, Princess Victoria. Edward was proud of his daughter, the future Queen Victoria, and proudly showed her off to an adoring public. In December 1819, Edward took his young family to a country house in Devon. There he developed the pneumonia that killed him in January 1820.

Duke of Kent. Below it are a large oak tree symbolizing Canada and three smaller oak trees representing the Island's three counties. All four trees rest on a single plot of land, symbolizing the fact that both PEI and Britain are islands.

In 2002, the Coat of Arms was amended to include a Royal Helm above the shield, upon which is perched a blue jay donning the royal crown of Prince Edward. Two silver foxes — one adorned in a wreath of potato blossoms and one wearing a fishing net necklace — support the shield. The foxes stand on a patch of grass sprouting a rose representing England, a thistle representing Scotland, a shamrock representing Ireland, a lily representing France and two Lady's Slippers, the provincial flower. Also prominent on the grass is an eight-pointed star, a Mi'kmaq sun symbol. The Island motto appears at the bottom.

Motto: *Parva sub ingenti* ('The small under the protection of the great')

Flag: The design of the flag is similar to that of the shield in the Coat of Arms, with the addition of a fringe of alternating red and white.

License Plates: Islanders can choose one of two license plates. One features Government House, the "Birthplace of Confederation," and the other, the Confederation Bridge.

The soil: The Charlottetown soil, designated the provincial soil in 1997.

Time zone: Atlantic

System of measurement: Metric

Voting age: 18

Our Namesake: Prince Edward Augustus, Duke of Kent and Strathearn

PEI POPULATION

With an estimated population of 146,283, PEI is home to 0.5 percent of all Canadians.

POPULATION IN PERSPECTIVE

The Island's population of just over 146,000 represents the smallest of the Canadian provinces, but is larger than the territories of the Yukon (33,144), the Northwest Territories (43,283) and Nunavut (31,448) all together. If PEI were an American state, it would be the smallest in population by far. Its closest contender, Wyoming, has about 3.8 times more people. On a global scale, PEI has approximately 126,000 more people than the small Pacific island nation of Nauru, while the population of China, the world's largest, is 9,513 times larger.

POPULATION DENSITY

With 23.9 people for each square kilometre, PEI is the most densely inhabited province in Canada. How does this stack up?

- Canada: 3.5 people/ km^2
- Nova Scotia: 17.3 people/ km^2
- New Brunswick: 10.2 people/ km^2
- Toronto: 866.1 people/ km^2
- Tokyo: 5,847 people/ km^2
- New York City: 10,194 people/ km^2

COUNTRY LIVING

Despite the relatively high population density of PEI, Islanders are among the most rural of Canadians. Nearly 45 percent of Islanders live in rural areas. Only Nunavut has fewer urban dwellers.

FAMILY STRUCTURE
- Number of Island children living in married two-parent households: 15,035
- Number of children living in common-law two-parent households: 1955
- Number of children living in female lone parent families: 5250
- Number of children living in male lone parent families: 1330

POPULATION BY AGE AND SEX

Age	Male	Female	Total
0-14	11,593	11,490	23,083
15–64	47,609	45,268	92,877
65+	11,911	14,297	26,208

Source: Statistics Canada.

POPULATION BY COUNTY

Kings County	17,745
Prince County	47,773
Queens County	83,765

GENERATION STATUS
- First generation Islanders: 4.5 percent
- Second generation Islanders: 5.7 percent
- Third generation or more: 89.8 percent

IMMIGRATION STATUS
- Percentage of immigrants who came to PEI before 1991: 69.9
- 1991 to 2000: 12.3
- 2001 to 2006: 17.8
- 2013 to 2014: 9.6

Source: Prince Edward Island Statistics Bureau

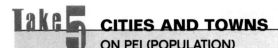

Take 5 CITIES AND TOWNS
ON PEI (POPULATION)

1. **Charlottetown** (64,487)
2. **Summerside** (16,488)
3. **Stratford** (8,574)
4. **Cornwall** (5,162)
5. **Montague** (1,895)

LANGUAGE

According to the most recent available data, percentage of the Island's residents whose mother tongue is:

English	93.3
French	4.0
Other	2.3

Source: Statistics Canada.

VITAL STATISTICS (JULY 2013-JUNE 2014)

Births	1,423
Deaths	1,306

Source: Statistics Canada.

LIFE EXPECTANCY

Average Lifespan	80
Men	78
Women	83

Source: Statistics Canada.

Did you know...

. . . that 31 Canadian cities — 13 of them in Ontario — have populations larger than PEI?

You know you are an

- You have fond memories of the phrase: "Please return to your vehicle for disembarkation."
- You only know what pop tastes like out of glass bottles.
- You've heard and uttered the phrase: "Shhhhh . . . the deaths are on!"
- You were a fan of Seaman's soda long before Pepsi bought it.
- You know what "covers the Island like the dew."
- You've seen the musical Anne of Green Gables 1,362,000 times . . . and counting.
- Your idea of a fast food sandwich is not a Big Mac or a Whopper — it's a Peter Pan burger.
- Your swimming lessons were at the beach.
- You prefer to go to the beach after Labour Day.
- You've had your fortune told by the creepy mechanical fortune teller guy at Rainbow Valley.
- You've visited a bootlegger on a Friday night.
- Your grandmother is a member of the Woman's Christian Temperance Union.
- You've never swam in a lake.
- You've had ADL concentrated milk, and you liked it.
- You have a "favourite" lobster supper vendor.
- Your car is a land yacht.
- Your yacht is a fishing boat.
- You learned to drive a tractor before you learned to drive a car.
- You remember getting in trouble for listening in on the party line.
- You've bet on a horse in the Gold Cup and Saucer race.
- You can drive from Summerside to Charlottetown without once driving on the TransCanada.
- You've never seen a traffic speed maximum sign greater than 90.
- Jellyfish don't creep you out - not even the red ones.
- You've gone on a pub crawl, led by Father of Confederation Leonard Tilley.
- When you jay walk – and you do it a lot – the police stop you, but just to ask how your father is keeping.
- You've never been in the deep woods.
- You know that the Red Bridge used to be green.
- You know a line of ten cars or more as "boat traffic."

Islander when...

- You think nothing of the fact that the two red mailboxes at the post office are labelled "Island" and "Away."
- You "slip" or "run" into town.
- You know everyone by their religious and political affiliations.
- You do not know route numbers, but you know each road by name.
- You think of a wake as "get to know your neighbours night."
- You know that PEI has three overpasses and one is a dead end.
- You have received letters of congratulation from the premier, the leader of the opposition, your local MLA and your MP for any number of your accomplishments.
- You know that there really was no Anne and that raspberry cordial has zero percent alcohol content.
- You use a down-filled comforter in the summer.
- You install security lights on both your house and garage door but leave both unlocked.
- You know that driving is better in winter because the pot holes are filled with snow.
- You know the difference between one long ring and one short ring, and two long rings.
- You travel an hour to see a movie.
- You had the same teachers your parents had when they went to school.
- You watch "mass for the shut-ins" just to see who's in church on Sunday.
- You know you could always get everything you wanted at Norman's, even on Sunday and holidays.
- The weather just isn't the weather without Boomer.
- You pronounce the word Island, "oisland", the word battery, "bachree," and the word wash, "worsh."
- You know the distinction between going "out west" and going "up west."
- You're sure you've seen the phantom ship of the Northumberland Strait.
- You think Moncton is a big city and Halifax is just freakin' huge.
- Your idea of a long drive is anything over an hour.
- You wonder what the big deal is about recycling – you've been doing it for years.

D – I – V – O – R – C – E

PEI has the second lowest divorce rate of any province in Canada after Newfoundland and Labrador.

Divorce per 100 marriages (rate by 30th anniversary)

PEI	Canada	NL (lowest)	Quebec (highest)
27.3	38.3	26.6	49.4

Source: Statistics Canada.

THE MARRYING KIND

Average rate of marriages for every thousand people on the Island is 6 – the highest rate in the country. Canada averaged a rate of 4.7, while Nunavut experienced the lowest rate in the country at 2.3.

FERTILITY

On average, women on PEI will have 1.47 children, slightly lower than the national average of 1.5. The average age of first time mothers on PEI is 28.2, just under the national average age of 29.0.

Source: Statistics Canada; Canadian Council on Social Development.

Take 5 TOP FIVE

BABY GIRL NAMES ON PEI

1. **Brooklyn**
2. **Olivia**
3. **Ellie**
4. **Madison**
5. **Claire**

AVERAGE HOUSING COSTS
Detached Bungalow
Summerside	$140,000
Charlottetown	$174,000

Standard Two-storey House
Summerside	$184,000
Charlottetown	$196,000

Luxury Condominium
Charlottetown	$300,000

Standard Townhouse
Summerside	$115,000
Charlottetown	$115,000

Source: Royal LePage, Survey of Canadian House Prices.

RELIGIOUS AFFILIATIONS OF ISLANDERS (PERCENTAGE)
- Roman Catholic: 47.4
- Protestant (United Church of Canada, Presbyterians, Anglicans, Baptists, Pentecostals and Lutherans): 42.8
- Eastern Orthodox Faiths, Muslims, Buddhists, Hindus and Jews: 5.0
- Of no religious affiliation: 4.8

Source: Statistics Canada.

Take 5 TOP FIVE MOST POPULAR
BABY BOY NAMES ON PEI

1. **Liam**
2. **Hunter**
3. **Connor**
4. **Jack**
5. **Jaxon**

Take 5 GODFREY BALDACCHINO'S
TOP FIVE PROS AND CONS OF THE
PRINCE EDWARD ISLAND "FIXED LINK"

Godfrey Baldacchino came to Prince Edward Island from the Island of Malta in 2003 to take up a Canada Research Chair in Island Studies at the University of Prince Edward Island. He has a strong interest in how islands and Islanders from around the world can learn from each other. Baldacchino is the author of *Bridging Islands: The Impact of "Fixed Links"* (Acorn Press, 2006).

Top 5 Positive Results of the Fixed Link:

1. The bridge brought oodles of dollars from Ottawa, including some 2,400 well-paying jobs at peak bridge construction in 1995. (Isn't that what 'Confederation' is all about for PEI?)

2. The bridge has attracted many, many more tourists, curious to experience the bridge; in the short term, a whopping half million more.

3. The bridge makes it much easier to ship to mainland markets such commodities as lobster, fish and mussels, as well as potato chips and aerospace components. Truckers are in high demand.

4. The existence of the bridge makes it more likely that immigrants (including other Canadians) will consider coming to, and settling down on, PEI.

5. Islanders can travel to shop in Moncton, New Brunswick with greater ease, speed and comfort. Islanders do this despite the fact that PEI, unlike New Brunswick, has no provincial sales tax on footwear and clothing.

Top 5 Negative Results of the Fixed Link:

1. Being now more accessible, PEI is increasingly in the sights of Americans who are priced out of beach houses in their own country. Although good news for the realtors and property sellers, this is bad news for the Island and Islanders long-term because the demand pushes up the general price of property for Island residents.

2. The bridge may have exacerbated the decline in the overall health of the Northumberland Strait, resulting in higher levels of particulate matter in suspension in the water, among other possibilities.

3. In making the Island "closer" to mainland Canada, PEI is now less exclusive to visitors. The bridge's 'novelty effect' in tourism has worn off, and visitation numbers are now to 'pre-bridge' (1996) levels.

4. Maritime Union is more likely. Geographically speaking, PEI is now a peninsula of New Brunswick.

5. Thanks to the hefty bridge toll, PEI is the only province in Canada where you still definitely have to pay to leave.

HEALTH CARE

- Number of hospitals on PEI: 7
- Number of physicians: 233
- Number working in the nursing profession: 1647
- Percent of province population covered by 9-1-1: 100
- Number of licensed ambulance vehicles: 16
- Number of EMS personnel: 100

Source: Government of Prince Edward Island; Canadian Institute for Health Information; Canadian Nurses Association.

EDUCATION

The Island's only university, the University of Prince Edward Island (UPEI), was established when the Prince of Wales College and St. Dunstan's University merged in 1969. There are, however, a number of curriculum-specific colleges on the Island.

The Atlantic Veterinary College in Charlottetown offers the only veterinary medicine program in Atlantic Canada. Holland College's Culinary Institute of Canada, Tourism and Culinary Centre, and Prince of Wales Campus are also located in Charlottetown.

Summerside boasts the College of Piping and Celtic Performing Arts of Canada, which specializes in the instruction of bagpipe and other traditional Scottish and Irish performing arts, including highland dance.

Did you know...

. . . that the fictional Cavendish birthplace of Anne of Green Gables receives three times more tourist visits than Charlottetown, birthplace of Canadian Confederation?

PUBLIC SCHOOL BOARDS
- English Language School Board
- La Commission Scolaire de Langue Française

THE PRESS
The main daily papers on the Island are Charlottetown's *The Guardian* and *The Journal Pioneer*, published in Summerside.

OTHER COMMUNITY NEWSPAPERS
West Prince Graphic (Alberton), *Cornwall Herald* (Cornwall), *Eastern Graphic* (Montague), *La Voix Acadienne* (Summerside)

OTHER PUBLICATIONS
Atlantic Fish Farming, Island Farmer, Island Classifieds, Coffee News PEI, PEI Buy, Sell and Trade, The Buzz, Voice for Island Seniors, Atlantic Pedaler Magazine, Heritage PEI Explorer's Guide, Island Fiddler Newsletter, Intuitive Times and *Island Magazine*.

Did you know...

. . . that the University of Prince Edward Island offers over $2 million in scholarships and awards each year?

RADIO

CBAF-FM-15	88.1 FM	Charlottetown	public news/talk (French)
CBAX-FM-1	88.9 FM	Charlottetown	public music (French)
CIOG-FM	91.3 FM	Charlottetown	Christian radio
CHLQ-FM	93.1 FM	Charlottetown	classic rock
CFCY-FM	95.1 FM	Charlottetown	country
CBCT-FM	96.1 FM	Charlottetown	public news/talk
CHTN-FM	100.3 FM	Charlottetown	adult contemporary
CBCH-FM	104.7 FM	Charlottetown	public music
CKQK-FM	105.5 FM	Charlottetown	CHR
CBCT-FM-2	92.3 FM	Elmira	public news/talk
CHTN-FM-1	99.9 FM	Elmira	adult contemporary
CKQK-FM-1	103.7 FM		CHR
CBPP	1490 AM	PEI National Park	tourist/park information
CBPP-1	1280 AM	PEI National Park	tourist/park information
CHTN-FM-2	89.9 FM	St. Edward	adult contemporary
CKQK-FM-2	91.1 FM	St. Edward	CHR
CBAF-FM-20	97.5 FM	St. Edward	public news/talk (French)
CBCT-FM-1	101.1 FM	St. Edward	public news/talk
CIOG-FM-1	92.5 FM	Summerside	Christian radio
CJRW-FM	102.1 FM	Summerside	classic hits
CBAF-FM-19	106.9 FM	Urbainville	public news/talk (French)

Weblinks

Government of PEI Home Page

www.gov.pe.ca

Your spot for one-stop shopping when it comes to PEI and all its offerings.

PEI Online

www.peionline.com

For Islanders and tourists alike. Check out a featured community and see what's going on around the Island.

Photos of PEI

www.gov.pe.ca/index.php3?number=81125

Maintained by the province, this page offers thousands of pictures in the form of images and video. Be sure to check out the live cameras and streaming radio broadcasts.

Place Names

Abrams Village (Prince): Settled in 1824, this Acadian community is named for one of its first residents, Abraham Arsenault.

Alberry Plains (Queens): This community, named in 1862, refers to the plentiful berry crops that thrive in the area.

Alberton (Prince): Once known as Cross Roads for the juncture of two trails, residents decided in 1862 to change the name in honour of Prince Albert who visited the Island two years earlier. Prince Albert later became King Edward VII.

Argyle Shore (Queens): Scots from Argylleshire first settled this area along the Northumberland Strait. Reminiscent of their homeland, inhabitants chose the name for their new home at a community picnic in 1847.

Bacon Cove (Queens): There's no porcine origin to this name. This cove at the mouth of Nine Mile Creek was named for Edward Bacon, Lord Commissioner of Trade and Plantations in the mid-18th century.

Basin Head (Kings): Site of a popular beach known for its "singing sands," the name describes the shape of the harbour.

Belfast (Queens): Originally home to an Acadian village, in 1803 it was settled by Thomas Douglas, the fifth Earl of Selkirk and several hundred Scottish settlers. Some say it is named for Belfast, Ireland, while others suggest the name is a corruption of the French, "La Belle Face."

Bonshaw (Queens): A Scottish immigrant in 1837 purchased 80 acres in Lot 30 and named his new farm after the Bonshaw Tower of his native homeland.

Charlottetown

European settlement here dates back to 1720 when nearby Port La Joie became the administrative centre of the then French-controlled Island. In 1763, England won the Island and two years later Samuel Holland surveyed it, recommending that a small community of 500 lots across the bay be made the capital of the British colony. He also proposed the name Charlottetown, to honour Charlotte, wife of King George III.

Not the most productive fishing harbour, Charlottetown's strength was its convenient location, just a short sail to the British stronghold of Nova Scotia and important routes to Halifax. The town grew slowly and in 1799 became a bonafide colonial capital when the Island was named after Prince Edward and received its independence from Nova Scotia. Charlottetown quickly became the business and administrative hub of the Island.

In 1855, Charlottetown was designated a city. Testifying to its resiliency, Charlottetown survived two major fires in the span of three decades, one in 1866 and one in 1884. In 1864, the city secured a place in the nation's history when it played host to the first round of Confederation talks, earning the nickname "the birthplace of Canada." The city may have been Confederation's nursery, but would not become a provincial capital until the Island joined Confederation in 1873.

At the time, Charlottetown was the 11th largest city in the young

Borden (Prince): On the Northumberland Strait, this town was originally called Carleton Point but was renamed in honour of Prime Minister Sir Robert Borden. Borden is the former home of the ferry terminal, the receiving end of the ferry route that once connected the Island to New Brunswick.

Brackley Bay/Beach (Queens): This area was named for Arthur Brackley, who arrived on PEI in 1770 and served as clerk of the young colony's Legislative Council until he accidentally drowned in 1774.

nation, a status it no longer enjoys. In 1995, the Charlottetown Areas Municipalities Act came into effect, expanding the city to incorporate Hillsborough Park, East Royalty, West Royalty, Winsloe, Sherwood and Parkdale. Despite this growth spurt, Charlottetown remains one of the smallest of Canadian capitals. With a population of fewer than 40,000 people, only Whitehorse (21,405), Yellowknife (16,541) and Iqaluit (5,236) are smaller.

Despite its small size, Charlottetown is a vibrant, modern centre. Home to government services, shopping, restaurants as well as the Island's sole university and the downtown and waterfront campuses of Holland College (the Island's community college) are also located in Charlottetown. The cultural scene is centered largely around the "Confed Centre," and the city remains, to this day, the urban hub of the Island and the destination for Islanders "going to town."

Though a definitively modern city, Charlottetown remains dedicated to its past, particularly to its Confederation connection. In 1993, George Street, home of the Province House National Historical Site, was designated a National Historic District. Each summer, actors dressed in period costume bring to life the personalities of key players in the Confederation talks as they guide visitors around the historic city.

Brudenell Point (Kings): The Brudenell River flows into Cardigan Bay and was named by Island surveyor Samuel Holland to honour George Brudenell, Earl of Cardigan.

Canoe Cove (Queens): Named after the French designation "Anse Canot," this place tenaciously clung to its name despite an effort to change it to Allen's Cove in 1765.

Cavendish (Queens): This farming settlement-cum-national park/tourist attraction was named for Field-Marshal Lord Cavendish by former Governor Walter Patterson (1735-1798) who owned this land, known then as Lot 23.

Cornwall (Queens): Now a booming suburb west of Charlottetown, this town was named in the late 18th century after the Duchy of Cornwall. Incorporated as a village in 1966, it amalgamated with Eliot River and North River in 1995, making a larger town of the same name.

Crowbush Cove (Kings): Now the site of one of the Island's best golf courses, this town was given the nickname of a one-time settler named John MacDonald. The moniker was a not-so-subtle reference to the shabby appearance of his farm.

Dalvay Beach/Lake/Pond (Queens): Known today as a summertime resort, this place got its start in 1895 when Alexander MacDonald of Cincinnati, Ohio — VP of the Standard Oil Company — built an elaborate summer home, naming it "Dalvay-by-the-Sea" after his home in Scotland.

Duvar (Prince): This community is named in honour of Scottish émigré John Hunter-Duvar who settled on PEI in 1857. A politician, Duvar was also a poet of considerable talent and had a wife with an intriguing and apparently secretive past; a note on Duvar's will suggests she might have been an illegitimate grandchild of King George III and Queen Charlotte.

Summerside

The first residents of the Summerside area were the Mi'kmaq who were joined in this Prince County locale by the Acadians in the 18th century. Around 1800, the first British settlers named a tiny village near the site Green's Shore after local English landowner, Daniel Green.

In 1840, the town got its current name when it was renamed for the licensed Summerside House Inn. Although it was named for the belief that the village occupied the sunnier southern shore of PEI, Summerside has not always enjoyed sunny times.

The young Summerside — incorporated as a town in 1877 — was built on shipbuilding, a lucrative but precarious industry. When the industry collapsed in the late 19th century, the town was sustained by agriculture. By 1910, sunnier days returned as Summerside became the centre of the Island's prosperous silver fox industry. Indeed, in 1920, the headquarters of the Canadian National Silver Fox Breeders' Association set up shop in the town.

In the 1940s, when the fur industry went the way of shipbuilding, WWII offered the town another new lease on life. In 1941, a Royal Canadian Air Force Station, which included the Air Navigational School — a training facility for NATO navigators — was constructed. Active during the war years, the base continued to bustle at war's end when new homes, roads and schools were built. The thriving military community was named Slemon Park. In the 1960s, RCAF Station Summerside was renamed Canadian Forces Base Summerside and became home to eastern Canada's 413 Search and Rescue Squadron. In its heyday, 1,400 people worked on the base.

In 1991, however, the town was dealt another blow with the closure of the base. Summerside was not to be beaten. Clouds of concern for the town's future parted when the former base was transformed into a successful business park bearing a familiar name. Slemon Park is now home to a number of innovative enterprises including companies involved in aerospace, commercial and light industries as well as Holland College's Atlantic Police Academy, Motive Power Centre, and Aerospace Centre.

Elmira (Kings): Located near Souris, this town was first known as Portage but was changed on the suggestion of local teacher George MacEachern. Elmira was the endpoint of the Island railway.

Glencoe (Kings): This community shares its name with a town in Scotland, the site of a 1692 massacre that saw 62 members of the Clan MacDonald slain by the Clan Campbell.

Harmony (Prince): As the story goes, this town was named for the fact that its ethnically diverse settlers got along peaceably, a rarity in Island settlements in the political tempest of the 19th century.

Indian River (Prince): A long-time Mi'kmaq settlement, the name could come from the fact that fishing rights for the river were reserved for the Mi'kmaq. The site is also home to the province's largest Catholic Church and is known for an annual summer music festival held in this acoustically stunning sanctuary.

Johnny Belinda Pond (Kings): Named in 1970, this name honours the play *Johnny Belinda*, which was based on the novel by Elmer Harris. Harris summered at Fortune Bridge and it was here that he first heard the story about a local deaf-mute girl who would become the subject of his well-known book.

Kensington (Prince): First known as Barretts Cross, the site of a tavern, the community was renamed in 1866 for the borough in London, England. Kensington was incorporated as a town in 1914.

Mermaid (Queens): First known as Mermaid Farm, it was named for the *HMS Mermaid*, a ship serving Port La Joie in the years 1764-65.

Mount Carmel (Prince): One of many Island place names derived from the Bible. The original Mount Carmel of *Old Testament* fame is where Elijah was asked to choose between God and Baal, and stems from the Hebrew word meaning "garden."

North Cape (Prince): This is the northernmost point of PEI. Cartier spied this area and called it "Savage Cape." The North Cape light warns mariners of the large rocky reef offshore, while North Cape's famed high winds have made it the site of the Atlantic Wind Test Site.

O'Leary (Prince): This community is named for an Irish settler, Michael O'Leary, and is home to the Island's Potato Museum.

Pipers Creek (Queens): This creek, which flows into Tracadie Bay, was first settled by the McInnes family, the kin of a well known piper, Michael McInnes.

Point Prim (Queens): Home to PEI's oldest lighthouse — built in 1845 — Point Prim is a corruption of the original French name, "Pointe à Prime."

St. Peter's Harbour (Kings): This site was home to the first unofficial French settlement in 1719. It was here that two shipwrecked French sailors settled and, despite their shaky start, saw Havre St. Pierre become a successful fishing village. The community was destroyed by the British in the 1758 deportation of Island Acadians, but was resettled in the 18th century by Scottish immigrants and then returned Acadians.

Scotchfort (Queens): This community was first settled by Captain John MacDonald, who purchased the land in order to settle Scottish emigrants. Upon landing at the site in 1772, the Scots discovered the ruins of an old French fort and the name was born.

Seacow Head (Prince): This region was named for the mammoth walrus that frequented the region and often left shed tusks behind as evidence. The walrus is now nearly extinct.

Victoria (Queens): This seaside fishing village, now a tourist town, was named in honour of Her Majesty, Queen Victoria.

Slang

Every country and region of the world has its own distinct language. Words and expressions have been nurtured and given meaning over time. They inform the jokes we tell and provide us with a shorthand that can only come to be known by living here. Prince Edward Island is blessed with a richness of language that can vary from county to county, and of which we can only offer a small sampling here.

Anchoring: A fisher's practice of storing lobsters in the water to keep them alive until processing.

Back door trots: The gastronomical affliction that causes one to run out the back door to seek relief in the outhouse.

Baking powder bread: Bread made with baking powder as a leavening agent, instead of yeast.

Baldy: A hornless cow.

Bare pole: Naked.

Bedlunch: A bedtime snack.

Bet: Past tense of 'beat' in terms of winning a game, as in "I bet you in the race!"

Boggie: One who lives in "the Bogs," a slum area of Charlottetown.

Clart: Dirty, messy person.

Coggly: Shakey or wobbly.

Cow's breakfast: A wide-brimmed straw hat.

Take 5 POET ANNE COMPTON'S FIVE
ISLAND WORDS OR PHRASES

Anne Compton is the Governor-General Award winning author of *Processional*. She was born and raised on the Island, and it informs all aspects of her work. In addition to the Governor-General Award, she is a two-time Atlantic Poetry Prize winner. Her most recent work is *Meetings with Maritime Poets: Interviews* (2006). She is the editor of *The Edge of Home: Milton Acorn from the Island* (2002) and co-editor of *Coastlines: The Poetry of Atlantic Canada* (2002).

Compton says as she has grown older, she dreams further back, recovering the language of her parents. Hers were born in 1903 and 1905. She says often the recovered words and phrases were ones associated with the daily objects or the routine activities of a household, which in her case was the farm.

1. **Stog:** A verb that refers to a vigorous stuffing or filling action. Brent MacLaine uses this word in his poem "Wintering"; people "stog rags" to stop up a draught.

2. **Fadder:** This was how my father referred to his father, a man who died before my birth, a stern man by all accounts. In its sound, it con-

Crack: Fart.

Dead man's overcoat: A coffin.

Dint: A dent in a bike or a car, such as one would get in a fender bender.

Done of it: Finished doing a task at hand.

Doozy up: To get dressed up to go out.

Downstreet: The main street or shopping district.

veys the sort of affection we more often hear in the various Victorian and Edwardian terms for mother.

3. **Headlands:** This is the turn-around area at the top of a field.
Perhaps it's still in use. You'd have to hear it as it was said decades ago — its two syllables run together. It's a term of vast metaphoric import, suggesting time as well as place, specifically that zone between life and death – one's last days or hours. Maybe Dante used it. I don't remember, but it has a liminal quality to it.

4. **Slurry:** A noun that identifies ice that is slushy, not quite frozen, the opposite of glib ice, which is especially hard and slippery.
Interestingly, both terms point to a cross-over from speech acts — slur and glib – to ice.

5. **Marragans:** This was a savoury, a kind of sausage really, made from the intestines of an animal at butchering time. The intestines were soaked, cleaned, dried, and stuffed with oatmeal and spices. My mother made marragans.

Flamer: A rough woman.

Fog: Commercially made bread.

Fox houses: The grandiose homes built by fox farmers in the early twentieth century heyday of this once-lucrative industry.

Friends of the Island: Islanders who opposed the Fixed Link on ecological and economic grounds.

From away: Someone from off the Island.

Government man: Someone who receives Employment Insurance.

Grunt: A steamed pudding made with berries, usually blueberries.

Hand socks: Mittens.

Haych: The eighth letter of the alphabet.

Islander: Someone from Prince Edward Island.

Islanders for a Better Tomorrow: Islanders who supported the construction of the Confederation Bridge.

Jigging clothes: Good clothing, but not your Sunday best.

Kit bag: A duffle bag or a gym bag.

Long liver: Someone with great longevity.

Lot: One of the 67 townships into which the Island was divided in 1767.

Maysil: A corrupted or Island-ized way to say "might as well."

Mail box money: Social assistance.

Mainlander: Someone who lives off the Island.

Mudder: One who digs mussel mud.

Newfoundland turkey: A seafood dinner.

Over across: Referring to a trip to the mainland or to someone or something coming from there, this term indicates just how remote the mainland was from the Island in the days before the bridge.

Oy-land/Oy-lander: An Islander's pronunciation of Island and Islander.

Pogey: Unemployment insurance.

Posy: An attractive young woman.

Sheep dung tea: Just what it says. This beverage has alleged medicinal properties to help when you feel baa-aa-aad.

Skin: When a man cruises for 'chicks.'

Slippy: Slippery.

Snollygoster: An unethical person.

Somewheres: Anyplace. "Did you see my keys somewheres?"

Spudhead: Someone from PEI, a reference to the preponderance of potato farms on the Island.

Stepmother's breath: A cool indoor draft.

Stormstayed: Snowed in.

Thra: A complainer who wastes time.

Up east: The most easterly part of PEI.

Where ya to?: Commonly asked instead of "where are you going?"

Whiff: To throw.

Zed cold: As cold as it can be.

Natural World

Covering 5,656 km², the province of Prince Edward Island is the smallest in Canada and accounts for 0.1 percent of its total land area. The next smallest province is Nova Scotia and it is larger than the Island by 50,000 km². In size, PEI edges out most of the Caribbean and South Pacific nations, and would rank 48th as a U.S. state, ahead of Delaware and Rhode Island.

A YOUNGSTER

Geologically speaking, PEI is a child. About 250-300 million years ago, deposited sediment formed the famous red sandstone that makes up the province's foundation. It was only about 15,000 years ago, however, when glaciers retreated and sea levels rose and made the province an Island.

LONGITUDE AND LATITUDE

Longitude: 63° W
Latitude: 46° N

On the global grid, Charlottetown is located at 46°17' N latitude and 63°8' W longitude. This places it on similar latitude lines with cities such as Seattle, Washington, Belgrade, Serbia and Ulaan Baatar, Mongolia, and on near-par longitude with Hamilton, Bermuda.

PHYSICAL SETTING

- Size: 5,656 km^2
- Length: 224 km
- Average width: 6-64 km
- Furthest distance from the ocean: 16 km
- Length of shoreline: 1,600 km

THE GULF OF ST. LAWRENCE

The Gulf of St. Lawrence is a huge 'mixing bowl' in which freshwater from the St. Lawrence River combines with the warmer water of the Atlantic. Added to the mix is the cold Labrador Current that streams in through the Strait of Belle Isle.

Influenced by these bodies of water, the Gulf is sometimes described as a large estuary. Its salinity levels range from 29-33 parts per thousand compared with the 33-37 parts per thousand found in the Atlantic. The Gulf's combination of warm and cold waters allow northern fish species to coexist with more temperate water species.

Due to the high abundance of food sources, the food web of the Gulf of St. Lawrence is impressive and ranges from tiny phytoplankton to the largest animal on earth, the Blue Whale.

Source: Geology of Prince Edward Island.

SEEING THE TREES FOR THE FOREST

Despite the fact that much of its coastline sports red or white sand beaches and that its fertile lowland topography is perfectly designed for

Did you know...

. . . that the sandstone bedrock beneath the Island is about 260 million years old?

agricultural use, PEI still has the lush productive forests so typical of the Canadian landscape. Approximately 257,000 hectares, or 45 percent of the Island is classified as forest, down from 48 percent in 1990. Abundant though it may be, the Island's treed acreage is declining as farms and cityscapes expand.

Source: Government of PEI — Agriculture, Fishery and Aquaculture.

WOODLAND

Percentage of PEI forest lands that is:
Softwood: 48
Hardwood: 52

MOTHER NATURE'S PRUNING

PEI rarely experiences the devastating fires that frequently ravage woodlands in other parts of the country. Because much of the province is settled, farmed or covered in beach sand, there are not enough forests to attract such large blazes. Most fires are reported as soon as the sparks begin to fly, giving fire fighters plenty of time to respond.

In most years, fires damage fewer than 100 hectares. The exceptions to this rule, however, were the years 1977 and 1986, when 1,200 hectares and 500 hectares were burned, respectively. Between 1991 and 2000, an average of 32 fires burned, taking 79 hectares of forest with them. The low figures have not always been the case. Back in 1960, the Portage fire wiped out nearly 7,000 hectares in Prince County.

FARM COUNTRY

Approximately 46 percent of PEI's 1.4 million acres about 594,000 acres in total, are cleared for farm use. The latest figures identify nearly 1,500 farms in the province. 3.7 % of the total population live on farms.

Source: Government of PEI — Agriculture, Fisheries and Aquaculture

BRIGHT RED MUD

Prince Edward Island is famous for many things: tubers, a big bridge and a redheaded girl named Anne. But one of the first sights that visitors marvel at is the "bright red mud" that Stompin' Tom turned into a folksong anthem.

The red of the soil – striking at any time of the day and stunning when accentuated by an Island sunset — is actually one of Mother Nature's many works in progress. The Island's bedrock is sedimentary, consisting mainly of soft, red sandstone. The soil contains phenomenally high concentrations of iron oxide, which, as it is exposed to air, oxidizes or 'rusts,' creating the gorgeous red and brown hues. The minerals and nutrients in this fertile red dirt are responsible for the Island's agricultural successes.

WATER, WATER, EVERYWHERE

With 1,600 km of coastline and more than 4,000 km of freshwater streams, the tiny Island seems absolutely drenched with water. It is ironic, however, because PEI has almost no naturally occurring freshwater lakes or ponds. While many of its streams carry the name 'river,' none actually have enough freshwater to deserve the title, and most morph into estuaries sooner rather than later.

Nearly 70 percent of the water in PEI's many streams comes from groundwater, the rest from rain and run-off. Despite all the water,

They Said It

" *[PEI] is one entire forest of wood; all the exceptions to the truth of this literally are not much more, even including the present clearance, than the dark spots upon the moon's face.* "
   – Walter Johnstone (1795-1824) – Scottish-born author of *A Series of Letters, Descriptive of Prince Edward Island* (1822) and *Travels in Prince Edward Island . . . in the years 1820-21* (1823)

PEI'S FIVE MOST COMMON
TREE SPECIES

1. Red Maple
2. White Spruce
3. Balsam Fir
4. Poplar
5. White Birch

flooding is rarely a problem on the Island. The small size and gentle currents of streams, combined with the Island's permeable soil, means that most of the water is absorbed. There is a downside, though, and that's the constant erosion of the soil.

Source: Government of PEI — Agriculture, Fisheries and Aquaculture.

CHARLIE VANKAMPEN'S
TOP FIVE PEI PLANTS

Charlie VanKampen is a partner in the VanKampen Greenhouses, an Island-owned and operated garden centre in Charlottetown that has been helping Islanders appreciate the greener side of life since 1959. Charlie weighs in on his picks for the province's top five plants, adding that at first they may constitute a "strange combination."

1. **The potato plant** – This is an easy one. We grow so many and, of course, it is the first thing people think of when they think of PEI.
2. **The Lady's Slipper** – The provincial flower.
3. **The Oak tree** – The provincial tree.
4. **Grass** – We lump all grasses together, though there are actually a large number of species and they all grow very well in our moist cool maritime climate. Grass is integral to all landscapes and helps colour the Island with manicured lawns, golf courses and pastures.
5. **Irish Moss** – The list would not be complete without a plant from the sea.

A RIVER RUNS THROUGH IT: THE HILLSBOROUGH RIVER

Although Prince Edward Island may be awash in water, very little of it is riverine. One example of this strange feature of the Island landscape is the Hillsborough River. Not quite a river (it is more of an estuary) the importance of this major waterway shouldn't be overlooked. The river is 45 km long, drains a 350 km^2 area (six percent of the province's landmass) and nearly splits the Island in two.

The Hillsborough River has contributed greatly to the Island's development, aiding and sustaining both its First People and Europeans alike, serving up an array of seafood, and providing an important travel route. It also provides a rich ecosystem, home to a vast range of wild-life including the great blue heron, bald eagles, muskrat, fox and more than 50 rare plant species.

In 1994, the province and the Hillsborough River Association nominated the river to the Canadian Heritage Rivers Systems in recognition of its importance to the Island, past and present.

Source: Canadian Heritage Rivers System.

SOIL EROSION

In its current conservation strategy, PEI environmental and govern-ment leaders acknowledge that soil erosion is the single most import-ant resource problem the province faces today. While freshwater streams trickle and meander slowly for much of the year, surface runoff from melting snow and ice can create quite a rush, taking with it a lot of soil. And that's in addition to the soil that's carried away throughout the year anyway thanks to wind and rain.

Did you know...

. . . that even a beached and dead Arctic Red Jellyfish can sting? So watch your step!

DANA GALLANT'S' TOP FIVE
MUST SEE BEAUTIFUL PEI REGIONS

Pedal and Sea Adventures is a small company run by one of Atlantic Canada's most experienced adventurers. Headed by adventure enthusiast Dana Gallant, Pedal and Sea Adventures has been organizing bike tours in Prince Edward Island for close to a decade. Gallant started Pedal and Sea so he could share one of the world's best places with travelers in need of a little R&R . . . riding and relaxation, that is!

1. Charlotte's Shore is the first region we encounter as we drive over the impressive Confederation Bridge. This year marks the 10th anniversary of this marvelous structure and this shore is a great introduction to the Island.

2. North Cape Coastal Drive is where we start our cycling portion of our tour in PEI. Nestled among the windmills, the North Cape Lighthouse is an impressive sight as we start our journey that passes secluded beaches and green fields and ends at PEI's trademark red cliffs towering over azure waters.

3. Anne's Land becomes our next beautiful area to cycle. This ride is always remembered for it's colourful fishing communities nestled amongst the fields of green.

4. Point's East Coastal Drive, the largest region of Prince Edward Island, is dotted with lighthouses and secluded beaches. We end the tour at the East Point Lighthouse after a day of feeling we were the only people on the road.

5. The province of Prince Edward Island itself and the people. You can't leave the province without your senses having been touched by its' natural beauty. There is a peaceful feeling that you have set your watches back 100 years and everything appears to be exactly as it should be. And the people there make sure nobody is left out from this happening to them.

SUN BLOCK

Dislodged soil is deposited along the streambeds, with heavier particles landing fairly quickly as sediment, and the lighter stuff making its way downstream to fall as silt and clay. All streams shoulder sediment and silt but when it overloads the stream, as is the case for many of the waterways on PEI, it's a recipe for environmental and economic disaster.

Sediment and silt block the sunlight required by aquatic plants and animals and they cloud water making it difficult for birds to hunt aquatic prey. The silt can also threaten fish-spawning habitats. It harbours bacteria and chemicals polluting the waters, detrimentally influencing the commercial fishery and shellfish industry.

Agriculture, too, is threatened as up to 14 tons of topsoil per acre can end up at the bottom of streams and estuaries each year. Ironically, it's agriculture itself that is the biggest culprit in the sad sand and silt saga. Farmers trying to squeeze as much growing space as possible out of their plots clear the land to the water's edge, removing the very vegetation that keeps the land and streams separate.

EROSION BY THE NUMBERS

- Because of climate change and global warming, sea levels around PEI are expected to rise between 30 and 110 cm by the year 2100.
- Average annual coastal erosion (for the last thousands of years): 0.5 m
- The estimated value of cottage property (within study area) lost to erosion between 1980 and 1990: $242,000 (or $22,000 / year)

Did you know...

. . . that despite common confusion, Great Blue Herons and Cranes are actually two very different species? Cranes are common to the northwest and only rarely venture into the Maritimes. You can spot the difference between the two by looking at their necks — when in flight, herons hold their necks in an 'S' shape while cranes fully extend their necks.

Take 5 — TOP ISLAND CAMPGROUNDS

1. **Brudenell River Provincial Park**
2. **Marco Polo Land**
3. **Mill River Provincial Park**
4. **Stanhope Campground**
5. **Twin Shores Camping Area**

Source: Government of PEI

- At current erosion rates, the percentage of cottage properties (within study area) that will be lost in the next 20 years: 10 percent
- Within the next century: 50 percent
- Average increase in sea level in Charlottetown over the last century: 32 cm; at Rustico: 29 cm
- Number of storm surges above 60 cm that occur each year in Charlottetown: 8
- Year by which a recent study by the Canadian Global Circulation Model indicates that the Gulf of St Lawrence could be ice free in the winter: 2045

Source: Government of Canada.

BEACHES

With a good portion of its 1,600 km shoreline jutting out into some of the warmest waters on the eastern seaboard, it's no wonder that many of PEI's most marketable assets are its beaches. The most popular beaches are on the coast of the Northumberland Strait, where shallow depths create some of the warmest waters north of Virginia and sandstone shores create white, sandy beaches.

Did you know...

. . . that the trees in which herons nest die as a result of their airborne tenants? The birds' excrement kills trees.

JELLYFISH

Most Island beach-goers have, at some point, come face to face with a jellyfish. The Gulf of St. Lawrence is home to two main types — the Arctic Red Jellyfish and the White Moon Jellyfish. The Arctic Red — also known as the Lion's Mane Jellyfish — is the larger and more common of the jellyfish duo. It is distinguishable not only by its rich purple colour, but also by its long red tentacles.

The Arctic Red uses these tentacles to stun its prey — zooplankton — but it won't discriminate and unwitting swimmers might also feel the wrath of the Arctic Red.

One who has a brush with these tentacles is rewarded with a mild stinging or burning sensation. Although it can be startling, the sting is harmless and easily remedied by rubbing sand on the affected area. The White Moon Jellyfish is less intrusive. A white translucent colour, this species has no tentacles and therefore cannot sting.

SEA GLASS

No day at an Island beach would be complete without a dip in the ocean or the building of a sand castle. Many Island beach visitors would add sea glass hunting to any list of 'must do' beach activities.

Sea glass is created from bottles or dishes that find themselves part of the ocean ecosystem. Over time, the motion of the waves and the friction of sand break up the glass, wearing smooth any sharp edges, leaving dainty coloured collectibles. Some sea glass has a frosty appearance, the result of a process by which the water removes lime and soda from the glass.

In this age of recycling and the use of plastics, it has become harder and harder to find an assortment of sea glass shades. Brown, whites and

Did you know...

. . . that the Canada Goose migrates to the south in the winter but occasionally 100 to 200 will winter right on the Island?

Take 5 — PEI'S TOP FIVE NATURAL
TOURIST ATTRACTIONS

1. **The beaches**
2. **The red cliffs**
3. **The quilt-like landscape**
4. **Scenic heritage roads** – the narrow red clay lanes that traverse the Island.
5. **The Hillsborough River**

Source: PEI Tourism

greens are fairly popular, but the once ubiquitous blue (for example, from Noxema bottles once made of glass) is much less common, and rarer still are shades of orange, red and yellow.

Source: North American Sea Glass Association

GREATNESS OF THE GREAT BLUE HERON

You do not have to be a "birder" to appreciate one of PEI's most majestic creatures, the Great Blue Heron, or *Ardea herodias*. These large birds stand an average 1.2 m, have wingspans of 1.8 m and can be spotted from March until late fall on the Island's coastlines and along inland waters where they dine on fish, frogs, snakes, mice and plants.

A third of Maritime Blue Herons summer on PEI. Although these birds often feed solo, the Great Blue Heron is a social bird. They are "colonial nesters," which means they live in large colonies — called

Did you know...

. . . that there are no official Crown lands on PEI? All lands owned by the provincial government were scooped up from the private sector through tax sales, land purchase programs and direct purchases from landowners.

1. **Piping plover**
2. **Smooth green snake**
3. **Pickerel frog**
4. **Red-bellied dace**
5. **Water shrew**

heronries — that are located away from human activity. Each year, PEI is home to an average 74 heron nests, made of twigs and built atop trees. For some reason, herons were especially fond of PEI in 1997. That year, the annual visitors built a record 507 nests.

Each season, a mother heron lays between three and five eggs, which take 28 days to hatch. Youngsters leave the nest approximately two months after hatching. To ensure future Island populations, efforts are made to maintain secure and peaceful nesting and feeding areas for the Great Blue Heron. It is illegal to hunt the bird both in Canada and the United States.

Source: Government of Prince Edward Island; Rickerts Nature Preserve.

PIDDLY PEAK

PEI is known for its rolling potato fields, not its mountain peaks. In fact, PEI ranks 13th in Canada for its provincial elevation. The highest peak reaches only 152 m and is located in the town of Springton.

Islanders can nevertheless try their skills at downhill skiing. Not a huge mountain, the ski facility of Brookvale Provincial Ski Park tops out at an elevation of 113 m and a vertical rise of 26 m.

Did you know...

. . . that there are no bears or moose on PEI?

Take 5 PEI'S TOP FIVE

RAREST PLANTS

1. Braun's Holly Fern
2. Round-leaved Dogwood
3. Whitlow Grass
4. St. Lawrence Aster
5. Black Ash Tree

GREAT WHITE

Deep in the waters off the coast of PEI lurks one of the earth's oldest and awe-inspiring creatures, the *Carcharodon carcharias*, better known as the Great White Shark. While the giant fish is rare in the North Atlantic and tends to remain well off shore in water reaching depths of 1,280 m, a record-making Great White was caught in Island waters. Fisherman off the coast of Alberton reeled in the largest Great White ever recorded in Canadian waters in August 1983. Estimated to be about 16 years old, this big girl was more than 5.7 m long.

Source: ReefQuest Centre for Shark Research; Canadian Shark Research Laboratory.

LOBSTER 101

Lobster suppers. Lobster key chains. Rubber lobsters. Lobsters are everywhere you turn on PEI. But how well do we really know the ubiquitous lobster? Lobsters are crustaceans, part of the phylum *Arthropodia*. This means they are from the same family as such unsavory creatures as spiders and cockroaches.

When they are freshly hatched, baby pea-sized lobsters float helplessly near the ocean's surface. Not surprisingly, only about 1 in a 1,000

Did you know...

. . . that it is actually a myth that the Lady's Slipper — the provincial flower — is protected by law? In truth, the flowers are common and it is legal to pick them.

survive their dangerous first month of life. Within a year, however, a surviving lobster will grow to about the size of your hand. As they grow, lobsters molt, shedding their shells to make room for larger ones. In fact, before it is five years old, a lobster can molt as many as 25 times!

As adults, lobsters live in dens on the ocean floor. There, these 'garborators' of the Atlantic gobble up garbage, such as dead fish and other rotting material. Lobsters are not picky eaters and, if push comes to shove, they even eat each other.

Lobsters are fiercely territorial and aggressive. When they are in the mood for love, however, they can be attentive and concerned crustaceans. Just after molting, a female chooses her mate. While her eggs develop, the soft-shelled female is protected in her mate's den until her new shell solidifies.

In nine to eleven months, the mother-to-be lays her eggs – as many as 20,000 of them – in a process that may take up to two weeks. Although lobsters face a dangerous first year of life, those who make it to maturity and who avoid lobster traps will probably live to a ripe old age; it is not uncommon for a lobster to live 20 or more years.

Did you know...

. . . that Brant (closely related to the Canada Goose) are one of the earliest migrants in the spring and live almost entirely on eel grass?

Weblinks

The Environment Coalition of Prince Edward Island

www.ecopei.ca

Find out more about the work of this community-based group working to improve the Island's environment since 1988.

The Macphail Woods Ecological Forestry Project

www.macphailwoods.org

Check out this website for information on the PEI conservation efforts and environmental research of the Environmental Coalition of Prince Edward Island and the Sir Andrew Macphail foundation. Book a tour or attend a workshop!

The PEI Potato Museum

www.peipotatomuseum.com

Potayto, Potahto! Curious about spuds? Check out the online exhibits of the Island's Potato Museum.

The Island Nature Trust

www.islandnaturetrust.ca

This not-for-profit group looks to protect the Island's natural areas.

Weather

Safer bets might be had at the track than laying money down predicting Prince Edward Island weather. Winds moving eastward from the interior of the continent combined with the mixing of major ocean currents make it a witch's brew that confounds even the best of meteorologists. The heating effect of the ocean in the southern Gulf of St. Lawrence and Northumberland Strait warms the province in the summer and autumn, cooling it in the spring and winter. Fall months on the Island are among the warmest in Canada.

In the winter, coastal ice conditions disable the moderating influence of the Northumberland Strait. The Island is infamous for winter storms. As winds whip snow, winter "white outs" are common and can create snow drifts metres high. Spring is often late arriving thanks to "drift ice" that lingers along the coast, cooling air temperatures. Summers are, however, worth the wait. Moderate summer months are warm and breezy. It's a good thing summers are not too hot — PEI has the highest humidity of any province.

AND THE WINNER IS . . .

- Record high: 36.7°C at Charlottetown on August 19, 1935
- Record low: -37°C at Bangor on February 7, 1993
- Record daily rainfall: 163.8 mm at Charlottetown, September 22, 1942
- Record daily snowfall: 86.8 cm at Charlottetown, February 17, 2015
- Record wind speed: 139 km/h at Charlottetown, September 30, 2003
- Record wind gust: 177 km/h at Charlottetown, December 19, 1963

Source: Environment Canada.

AVERAGE ISLAND TEMPERATURES (°C)

Jan	Feb	Mar	Apr	May	Jun	Jul	Aug	Sep	Oct	Nov	Dec
-7.5	-7.3	-2.8	3.1	9.6	14.9	18.9	18.6	14.0	8.4	2.9	-3.9

Coldest month: January

Warmest month: July

PRECIPITATION

- Total annual precipitation: 1078 – 1240 mm
- Rain: 797 – 963 mm
- Snow: 216 – 316 cm

Source: Environment Canada.

GROWING SEASON

The Island climate is great for potatoes. PEI has on average 130 frost-free days each year between May and October, and mild falls allow for an extended harvesting season.

Did you know...

. . . that the term "August Gale" now refers to any late summer storm on PEI, but specifically harkens back to the storm that buffeted the Island on August 24, 1873?

Take 5 FIVE INFAMOUS HURRICANES
AND TROPICAL STORMS
(IN ORDER OF WIND STRENGTH)

1. **Hurricane Juan**, Category 2, September 29, 2003
2. **Hurricane Ginny**, Category 2, October 29, 1963
3. **Hurricane Unnamed**, Category 1, August 27, 1924
4. **Hurricane Unnamed**, Category 1, August 15, 1891
5. **Tropical Storm Cindy**, July 12,1959

WIND AND MORE WIND

The average annual wind speed on the Island is 18.8 km/h, the second highest in Canada. It also has the second windiest summers, when winds average 16.5 km/h, and the second windiest winters, with wind speeds averaging 20.49 km/h. The Island has 56.67 "windy" days each year, the third highest in Canada.

Source: Environment Canada; Wind Energy Institute.

THE FURY OF JUAN

September 29th, 2003, is a date that Islanders will not soon forget. That night, the Island was buffeted by the now-infamous Hurricane Juan. When Juan first made landfall off Nova Scotia, it was a category 2 storm, rare for the north Atlantic. Although the storm's strength had diminished by the time it reached PEI, Juan still packed a powerful punch. After crossing the Northumberland Strait, which at 18°C was three degrees warmer than normal for that time of year, Juan hit PEI at 3am following a northwest beeline path that took the storm from the Confederation Bridge to the Gulf of St. Lawrence.

Juan's highest winds reached 139 km/h in Charlottetown, causing much damage. Juan's destructive winds tore roofs off buildings, uprooted enormous old trees and left two-thirds of the Island without power. The cost of damages totaled in the millions. As a testament

They Said It

to the fury of Juan, this name has been retired from the hurricane naming system.

Source: Environment Canada; National Hurricane Centre.

HURRICANES

Despite the impact of the Hurricane Juan, hurricanes are actually rare events on PEI. In the past 103 years, only five hurricanes have hit the Island.

THE YANKEE GALE

Although PEI is known as the "Garden of the Gulf," one storm in October 1851 turned Island waters into the "Graveyard of the Gulf." The lethal storm — known as the Yankee Gale — left a path of destruction across the Island, striking the north shore with particular ferocity.

In the mid-19th century, it was common for New England fishing fleets to gather in the Gulf of St. Lawrence off PEI's north shore to fish rich mackerel stocks. These "Yankee" fishers bore witness to the dreadful storm that raged from October 3rd to 5th.

Tossed like corks on massive swells in the unrelenting wind, their boats' masts and sails were ripped away, leaving the fishers exposed to the wrath of an angry sea. The toll was 100 ships and as many as 250 lives lost.

For weeks after the storm, bodies washed up on the Island's north shore. Islanders were afraid to walk their beaches for fear of discovering victims' remains. Their identities may be lost in time, but memories of the sad fate of the Yankee sailors live on in stories of the storm that bears their name.

Take 5 LINDA LIBBY'S FIVE EXTREME
ISLAND WEATHER EVENTS

Linda Libby has been an Environment Canada employee for over 20 years. Initially employed as weather technician, Linda became a weather forecaster in 1990. Her work with Environment Canada has allowed Linda to work from Newfoundland to Alberta. Returning to the Maritimes in 2002, Linda has been the Environment Canada's Weather Preparedness Meteorologist for PEI since September 2006.

1. **Hurricane Juan**, September 28th-29th, 2003: Quite literally this storm re-shaped the surroundings of many Islanders.

2. **White Juan**, February 18th, 2004: With this wintery blast, 74.4 cm of snow fell in Charlottetown shattering the old record of 50.8 cm from 1926.

3. **Storm Surge**, January 25th-26th, 2000: High water levels associated with a low pressure system significantly damaged the sand banks and shoreline in the Souris area. With rising water levels due to climate change, this type of damage is expected to become more frequent. This was the first of several such events recorded in the early 2000's.

4. **Ice Storm**, March 31st, 2003: This weather system produced freezing rain and ice pellets that led to downed power lines in PEI, especially over Prince County. Some residents were without power for more than five days. Elsewhere on the Island, rain and high water resulted in road damage.

5. **Blizzard of '82**, February 20th-21st, 1982: Islanders that I have talked to indicate that parts of Prince county were literally cut off from the rest of the Island for days as the only road was not passable. Strong winds after the initial snowstorm produced intermittent blowing snow conditions for several days.

1. **-37.0 C°** on February 7, 1993 in Bangor
2. **-33.3 C°** on January 12, 1976 in New London
3. **-33.0 C°** on February 27, 1990 in Alberton
4. **-30.6 C°** on February 19, 1973 in Monticello
5. **-30.6 C°** on January 18, 1923 in Charlottetown

RAIN, RAIN

The Island has 5,037 hours of cloudy skies each year, making it the third cloudiest province in Canada. On an average of 7.11 days each year, the Island is soaked by more than 25 mm of rain, making it the third wettest province. Island crops receive over 841 mm of rain each year, again giving the Island a third place weather finish. On September 22, 1942, Charlottetown recorded 163.8 mm of rain, the greatest daily total ever recorded on PEI.

Source: Environment Canada.

SPUD MUD

No Islanders are more attuned to the weather than the farmers. The wet weather in the autumn of 2006 really put a damper on the potato harvest. That October, a month that usually sees a rainfall of 109 mm, saw nearly twice that amount fall. Over 216 mm drowned farmers' fields. More than half of PEI's potato growers struggled to harvest their potatoes from the "Spud-Mud" by Halloween, the typical target date for completion of the harvest.

Many tractors were stuck and conditions seemed ripe for blight and other plant diseases. Fortunately, temperatures remained unusually mild and the sun shone down on the fields a few days before the 31st deadline. This allowed the potato farmers to recoup some losses. A full 30 percent of the potato yield was lost.

Source: Government of PEI.

Take 5 — TOP FIVE HOTTEST DAYS
IN PEI HISTORY

1. **August 19, 1935**   36.7°C, in Charlottetown
2. **August 13, 1944**   36.1°C, in Alliston
3. **May 22, 1977**   36.1°C, in Tignish
4. **August 12, 1944**   34.4°C, in Charlottetown
5. **August 10, 2001**   34.0°C, in New Glasgow

LIGHTNING

On average, PEI has 11.15 days each year with thunderstorms, the sixth fewest in Canada.

Source: Environment Canada.

FOG

PEI gets fog on an average 40.45 days each year, making it the fourth foggiest province in Canada. Compared to those in other eastern Canadian communities, Island fog lights are not used that much. Summerside sees on average 37 days of fog and Charlottetown 44, a far cry from other Atlantic Canadian cities such as St. John's, Halifax, and Saint John, which see 119, 101 and 106 days of fog, respectively.

Source: Environment Canada.

LIGHTHOUSES

Currently, there are 47 lighthouses on PEI. Architect Isaac Smith, the same man who designed Province House, designed the Island's first lighthouse in 1845.

Source: InfoPEI.

Take 5 — FIVE FAMOUS SHIPWRECKS

OFF PEI

1. *The Marco Polo*, July 22,1883
2. *The HMCS Assiniboine*, November 10,1945
3. *The HMS Phoenix*, September 12,1882
4. *The Fairy Queen*, October 10,1853
5. *The Welcome*, August 29,1883

PERFECT SUMMER DAY

- The Island has only 0.84 days on average each year where temperatures exceed 30°C.
- PEI receives 1,905 hours of bright sunshine, approximately 150 days, each year.

Source: Environment Canada.

IT'S NOT THE HEAT

- Prince Edward Island has the most humid summers in Canada. The average hourly vapour pressure in June, July and August is 1.52 kPa.
- Charlottetown has a 21 percent chance that the humidex will be above 30°C on a July afternoon. The highest recorded humidex was 41°C on August 15, 2002.

Source: Environment Canada.

Did you know...

... that White Juan dropped an estimated 6,000,000 tonnes of snow on PEI?

PASS THE SHOVEL

- Up to 30 percent of all precipitation falls as snow and the white stuff falls an average 48 days a year.
- The Island gets more than ten cm of snow on about 8.16 days each year, making it third in the country in terms of heavy snowfalls.
- The Island receives on average 296.07 cm of snow each winter, making it the fourth snowiest province in Canada.
- In the spring, the Island gets on average 81.95 cm of snow, making it the third snowiest province in the spring.
- The Island endures 22.54 days of blowing snow each year, the fourth highest in Canada.
- All this snowy news has a silver lining. While it may come often, snow does not last on PEI. With snow on the ground for 121 days a year, PEI has the shortest spell of snow cover in all of Canada.

Did you know...

. . . that on PEI there is a type of snow known locally as 'snirt'? It's a mixture of 'wind blown' snow and red PEI mud.

Did you know...

. . . that for many Islanders the abbreviation "PEI" has a far more apt and jarring meaning? Given the insidiously bumpy roads with which Islanders must contend, especially in the spring, "Potholes Every Inch" seems appropriate.

1. **86.8 cm** on February 17, 2015 at Charlottetown
2. **74.4 cm** on February 19, 2004 at Charlottetown
3. **50.8 cm** on February 5, 1926 at Charlottetown
4. **48.8 cm** on March 7, 1999 at Alberton
5. **47.5 cm** on February 7, 1956 at Charlottetown

DREAMING OF A WHITE CHRISTMAS

A white Christmas is defined as two cm or more of snow cover on the ground on December 25th. The odds of having a white Christmas in Charlottetown stand at 87 percent. The probability of a "perfect Christmas," defined as snow in the air and at least two cm on the ground, is less, at 48 percent.

The greatest snowfall ever on Christmas day in Charlottetown was 19.3 cm in 1970.

BLINDING BLIZZARD

Islanders will not soon forget February 1982. From the 22nd through to the 26th, a mammoth snowstorm dumped 60 cm of snow and whipped up 100 km/h winds, which resulted in zero visibility and wind chills of -35°C. The Island was paralyzed for a week. Cars, trains and even snowplows were buried in five- to seven-metre drifts, and the province was cut off from the mainland.

Source: Environment Canada.

Did you know...

. . . that PEI has the second warmest autumn months? Only Nova Scotia's falls are warmer.

THE GREAT ICE STORM OF 1956

PEI has the dubious distinction of getting more freezing rain than any other province. Freezing rain falls on an average 16.51 days a year, often paralyzing the Island. The ice storm of 1956 was especially bad. The ice began falling on January 5th and continued to coat the Island for two days. Trees were snapped and power and telephone lines felled as damages topped out at $2 million. The whole western portion of the province lost power. A state of emergency was declared in Summerside and, amazingly, it was not until June that the last of the outages were repaired.

Source: If You're Strong Hearted: Prince Edward Island in the Twentieth Century; Environment Canada.

"WHITE JUAN": THE BLIZZARD OF '04

A weather bomb dropped on PEI on February 19, 2004 and the explosion reverberated for three days. During that period, a blizzard hammered the Island, dumping 74.4 cm of snow and bringing winds of more than 100 km/h. A state of emergency was declared when snow-plows could not keep the roads open.

Damaged trees were easily felled by the storm and toppled onto the power lines. As many as 12,000 customers were left in the dark when the main power transmission line was damaged by the gusts. The Confederation Bridge was closed for the second time since its opening, and it was weeks before all Island roads were passable. A chorus of storm surge warnings were issued and children rejoiced in the many school cancellations. Because it followed just a few short months after Hurricane Juan had blasted the province, this ferocious winter storm became known as "White Juan."

Source: Environment Canada.

WINTER OF OUR DISCONTENT

A late April storm in PEI helped the winter of 2014-15 break the record for most snowfall recorded in one year on Prince Edward Island-more than the previous record of 539 cm set in 1971-72. 551 cm in total fell during the winter of 2014-15, an all- time high. During this winter, PEI also set a record of 159cm of snow on the ground for the month of March, breaking the 1956 record of 122cm. A storm on February 16th brought 86.8 cm of snow, with winds gusting to 128/kph, making it a more severe storm than White Juan.

ICE TYPES

- Board ice: Solid sheets of ice that extend from the shore into open water.
- Cat ice: Shell ice; thin ice covering an air pocket from which water has retreated.
- Drift ice: A piece of floating ice driven by winds and currents.
- Ice Cake: A large piece of floating sea ice.

Weblinks

Island Cams

www.gov.pe.ca/islandcam/index.php3

Want to see what the weather and road conditions are like on PEI? See for yourself by viewing conditions as recorded by one of PEI's "Island cams."

Wind Energy Institute of Canada

www.weican.ca

If climate change, global warming and alternatives to fossil fuels are of interest to you, find out all you need to know about the experimental wind farm located in the most western part of the province, with its superb 300 degrees of glorious vista exposure to the Gulf of St. Lawrence.

Island Lighthouses

www.tourismpei.com/island-lighthouses

If you are interested in seeing many of the historic lighthouses on the Island, this site is for you. Find a useful reference with maps and directions for most major lighthouses at this site.

Crime and Punishment

CRIME LINE

1752: St. Germain dit Perigord is put to death by Mi'kmaq who blame him for the devastation of crops by plagues of mice.

1763: The Royal Proclamation brings to the Island the severe heritage of British Criminal Law.

1778: First sentence of death is passed on Elizabeth Mukely for theft. She escapes the gallows because no one will hang a woman.

1792: "An Act Relating to Treasons and Felonies" defines those offences punishable by death.

1792: Joseph Farrow is hanged for the rape of a 12-year-old girl in the Island's first public execution.

1792: Donald McIntyre is the first to be flogged under the new act for committing a series of petty larcenies.

1813: John Nicholson and his son Samuel are hanged for the murder of John Ross, whom they beat to death with their fists and muskets.

1815: Brothers Sancho and Peter Byers, two Black residents of PEI, are hanged for theft connected to two separate incidences. Peter stole 5£, while Sancho robbed a woman.

1821: James Cash is hanged for rape and James Christie for theft.

1836: The Island's 1792 version of British law is replaced and older forms of punishment, such as whipping and the pillory, are replaced by prison terms.

1869: George Dowey is hanged for murder.

1888: William Millman is hanged for murder.

1900: "An act prohibiting the sale of intoxicating liquor," the Island's first Prohibition Act, also known as the Scott Act, is passed. It prohibits the manufacture and sale of alcohol but allows alcohol to be sold under a physician's prescription for medicinal use. Cough, cough.

1918: The Prohibition Act is completely re-written. New legislation provides for the establishment of a six-member Board of Commissioners to be appointed for a three-year term by the Lieutenant-Governor-in-Council to administer the Act. The Commission is empowered to license one wholesale vendor and as many retail vendors as deemed necessary.

1941: Fred Phillips and Earl Lund are hanged for the murder of Peter Trainor. The duo's deaths are PEI's last hangings.

1945: An amendment marks the beginning of the end of Prohibition. This amendment states that, provided a physician felt that the use of liquor over an extended period would benefit the health of a patient, he could prescribe 26 oz of spirits, or 104 oz of wine, or nine full quarts of ale, to be delivered weekly to a "patient" over a six month period.

1948: The "Temperance Act" is introduced, repealing of the Prohibition Act and establishing a Government Liquor Control System similar to the other provinces. PEI is the last province to repeal prohibition.

1988: A bomb explodes in the Law Courts in Charlottetown and police begin their search for the bomber who would taunt them for 13 months and detonate another explosion.

First Death Sentence

Joseph Farrow was the first person put to death by court order on PEI. He was arrested on July 14th, 1792, tried on July 20th, and hanged the same year. The indictment against him read "not having the fear of God before his eyes, but moved and seduced by the instigation of the devil, [Farrow] did ravish and carnally know one, Elizabeth Beers, contrary to the statute and the peace and dignity of the king." The victim was just twelve years old.

The jury found him guilty and he was sentenced to hang publicly. One juror worried about what would become of Farrow's wife and three small children and said, "We must maintain them and I will give her a cow and a calf." He never did make good on his promise. Farrow's widow, Judith, subsequently remarried an Island farmer, John Gouldrup whose name was later abbreviated to Gould. She became the great grandmother of Jacob Gould Schurman, one-day president of Cornell University.

1991: RCMP arrest the ship *NicNac* off Clearwater on the North Coast of Prince Edward Island and make a massive drug bust.

1997: Roger Charles Bell, the PEI Bomber, is arrested and subsequently sentenced to 12 years after pleading guilty.

2000: Fred Sheppard is sentenced to ten years for manslaughter in the killing of his common-law partner, Kimberly Ann Byrne.

2009: PEI Supreme Court and Court of Appeals become separate divisions, effective January 1st.

2014: Prince Edward Island senator, Mike Duffy, was charged with 31 criminal offenses, including fraud, breach of trust and bribery. He had quit the Conservative caucus in 2013 amid this scandal. After sitting as an independent for a short while, he was suspended without pay for two years.

EARLY LAW AND ORDER

PEI's early legal system was based on England's 'Bloody Code.' It distinguished two categories of offences: felonies, which usually carried the death penalty, and misdemeanors which were punishable by whipping, exposure in the stocks or pillory, maiming or exile.

Some Island offenders who were sentenced to death were given the option of 'Benefit of Clergy,' which meant they were conveyed to ecclesiastical authorities for punishment. These offenders escaped the gallows but were branded on the thumb with a "T" for thief or an "M" for murderer. This system of law remained in effect on PEI until 1836 when the older forms of punishment were replaced by jail sentences.

PAINFUL PERJURY

In 1792, the penalty for perjury was severe. The offender was placed in the pillory, his ears then removed and nailed to the wood beside him.

THE LAST DEATH SENTENCE

The last public hanging in PEI occurred on April 6th, 1869 (the actual last hanging — not open to the public — didn't happen until 1941). George Dowey was a sailor from Montreal who had sailed from New Orleans to Boston and from London to the Black Sea. He admitted that he had led a "wild and reckless" life and that he had an "unholy passion" for women.

Rum-Running in PEI

In 1901, PEI became the first province to enact Prohibition. This law made it illegal to manufacture, sell or possess intoxicating alcohol. Despite harsh fines and the threat of impounded ships, rum running became a lucrative way of life for poor Islanders during the Prohibition years. Ed and John Dicks from Georgetown were the Island's most famous rum runners, and both captained the notorious rum running schooner, the Nellie J. Banks.

For twelve years, this little ship carried alcohol to and from the province, eluding authorities who patrolled the waters extending three miles off the Island's coast. Finally, on August 6th, 1938, the government cutter Ulna caught up to the Nellie J. Banks. She was seized and ignominiously sent off to Charlottetown. The Nellie J. Banks had made her last run.

Later that year, the three-mile limit was extended to twelve — no longer did the fishermen keep a close watch on the horizon for the little "whiskey boat." A ditty, credited to Clinton Morrison Sr., has survived to express the joy and anticipation felt by thirsty Islanders when the little schooner came to shore.

It was the twenty-fourth of May
The sky was bright and clear
A shout went up from man to man
The NELLIE BANKS is here!

When John Cullen, a sailor from Liverpool, approached his girlfriend, a drunk and jealous Dowey pulled a sheaf knife and stabbed him in the heart.

At his trial, Dowey's girlfriend learned of his wife in Ireland. Out of revenge the crossed lover withheld the crucial evidence that Cullen had grabbed Dowey by the throat and that this act led to the stabbing in self-defense.

Dowey was convicted of murder and sentenced to hang. On April 6th, 23-year-old Dowey went to the gallows. For more than a half hour before his execution, the marked man addressed the crowd, confessing that "during all my voyages and when I was in port, there was no sin of which I was not guilty." The noose was then placed around his neck. Expecting his imminent death, the drop opened – but the rope snapped.

Dowey fell, very much alive, sixteen feet to the ground. He was taken back to his cell until a new rope was found. For the second time in one day, Dowey was placed in position and the drop opened.

This time, the rope detached from the cleat and he crashed to the ground again still alive. But Dowey was not to get a third trip to the scaffold. Enlisting help from some constables, the sheriff hoisted Dowey and he was left hanging for some forty minutes before being pronounced dead by the medical examiner.

ELIZABETH MUKELY

On February 21st, 1778, Elizabeth Mukely received the Island's first death sentence. She was employed as a domestic servant by Gideon Ticeborn from whom she stole seven pounds and seven shillings. In sentencing, the Chief Justice recommended that she repent and give "an entire attention to preparing herself for going out of this world in a short time as her life was the only atonement she could give by the laws of her country for her fatal fault."

Fortunately for Mukely, no hangman who would slip the noose around the neck of a woman could be found on the Island, in spite of the promise of five pounds to anyone who would. Tom Mellish, the Provost Marshall, refused to do it and as a result was forced to resign his position. Most Islanders agreed with Mellish and no woman was ever hanged on PEI. Women sentenced to death received 'royal mercy' and escaped the gallows.

Minnie McGee: Murderous Mother

Minnie McGee was the mother of eight children under the age of thirteen. In mid January of 1912, her three-year-old and her one-year-old both died of a fever.

On April 11th of the same year, Mrs. McGee and her children — with the exception of Johnny, aged 10 — sat down to a supper of herring, corn bread and tea, after which the children became violently ill. All five were dead within twenty-four hours, and when Provincial Health Officer Dr. W. J. MacMillan arrived on the scene, he found the children lying side by side in the parlour. Although ptomaine poisoning was initially suspected, it was later discovered that all had died of phosphorous poisoning at the hand of their dinner-preparing mother.

At trial, testimony was heard that Mrs. McGee had bought twenty-one gross of kitchen matches and had administered the phosphorous in sugar water. After the funeral, her husband, a man well known for being abusive, returned to work in Sturgeon, leaving ten-year-old Johnny with his mother. She bought more matches and Johnny became her sixth victim.

Minnie McGee was convicted only of Johnny's murder and sentenced to death by hanging on July 22nd, 1912. On hearing her sentence, she cried out, "Hanged! Hanged! Hanged, hang me now and be done with it!" The sentence, however, was never carried out because the jury judged her insane and recommended mercy. Her sentence was commuted to life in prison. She died on January 11th, 1953, having spent over forty years in prison and psychiatric detention.

CRIME ON PEI

In 2014, PEI recorded 6,246 Criminal Code offenses per 100,000 people. This is considerably fewer than the 47,332.1 offenses per 100,000 people living in the Northwest Territories, the jurisdiction with the highest rate of Criminal Code offenses in the country.

MURDER

Today PEI has a murder rate of 0.69 per 100,000 people, compared to the rate of 22.5 per 100,000 people recorded in Nunavut, the highest rate in Canada.

ROBBERY

PEI's robbery rate rests at 15.84 incidences per 100,000 people. The rate in Manitoba is more than ten- fold higher at 179.1 per 100,000.

MOTOR VEHICLE THEFT

The rate of auto theft on PEI is 82.62 per 100,000. The highest rate, also found in Manitoba, stands at 1,236.3 per 100,000 people.

YOUTH CRIME

- Number of youth cases tried in PEI: 178
- Number resulting in convictions: 57%
- Number acquitted: 1%
- Number stayed: 42%
- The incarceration rate per 10,000 young persons (2013): 5.24
- Total actually incarcerated: 8.0
- Probation rates per 10,000 young persons: 112.3
- Number actually on probation: 116

Source: Statistics Canada.

Take 5 TOP FIVE MOST COMMON CRIMES COMMITTED ON PEI

1. **Theft under $5,000**
2. **Assaults**
3. **Traffic violations under the Criminal Code, including impaired driving**
4. **Break and enter**
5. **Fraud**

Source: Statistics Canada.

COUNTING COUNTERFEITING

- Total number of fake banknotes passed and seized in Canada in 2014: 62,418
- Total number of fake banknotes passed and seized in Canada in 2007: 13,960
- Number passed and seized in Prince Edward Island in 2014: 165

Source: RCMP.

IMPAIRED DRIVING

PEI records a rate of impaired driving of 307.05 per 100,000 people which is less than a quarter the rate of 1,801.3 per 100,000 people recorded in the Northwest Territories (the nation's highest). Impaired driving is a crime that results in jail time for Island offenders more often than in any other Canadian province. A full 85.7 percent of all Island impaired driving convictions ended in incarceration, the highest rate in Canada. Newfoundland and Labrador, the province with the second highest rate, saw only 26.3 percent of such cases end with jail sentences. There were a total of 241 impaired convictions in 2014.

DRUG OFFENSES
- Drug offenses in Prince Edward Island: 183.15 per 100,000 (lowest in Canada)
- In NWT: 1,050.83 per 100,000 (highest)

POLICE OFFICERS
- Canada: 68,896
- Number of officers on the Charlottetown City Police Force: 53
- Number of regular RCMP officers on Prince Edward Island: 141
- Number of civilian members: 14
- Number of municipal police: 90

Source: Statistics Canada and City of Charlottetown.

CORRECTIONAL FACILITIES
- PEI is home to two adult correctional facilities: the Provincial Correctional Centre in Charlottetown and the Prince County Correctional Centre in Summerside.
- Young offenders are housed at the PEI Youth Centre in Summerside.

POLICING PEI
- Per capita cost of policing on PEI, the lowest in Canada: $157
- In Nunavut, the highest in Canada: $688
- Number of police officers per 100,000 people on PEI: 166
- In the Northwest Territories, the highest in Canada: 419
- In Alberta, the lowest in Canada: 163
- In Italy: 556
- In Finland: 156
- Percentage of police officers on PEI who are female, the second lowest in Canada: 12.6
- In Nunavut, the lowest in Canada: 10.1
- In Quebec, the highest in Canada: 21.8

SENTENCING

- Median prison sentence in PEI, the lowest in Canada (tied with Alberta): 15 days
- In Quebec, the highest in Canada: 90
- Percentage of defendants found guilty in PEI who were sent to prison: 71.1
- In New Brunswick, the highest in Canada: 79.9
- In Ontario, the lowest in Canada: 59.8

Source: Statistics Canada.

FINES FOR CRIMES
Speeding

• 1st offence	$100-200
• Subsequent offences	$200-400
• Speeding in a municipality	$50-200
• Subsequent offences	$100-400
Slow driving	$100-500
Illegal parking	$50-100

Source: Government of Prince Edward Island.

THE CHARLOTTETOWN BOMBINGS

Early one October morning in 1988, a bomb exploded in the Law Courts in Charlottetown, causing extensive damage to the law library. Fortunately, because it was just six o'clock a.m., the building was empty and no one was hurt.

On April 20th, 1995, just one day after the terrorist bombing in Oklahoma City, another explosion rocked the PEI Legislature sending shrapnel several blocks and blowing out twenty windows.

On May 24th, a letter addressed to the Chief Justice of the Island claimed responsibility for the bombings. Emblazoned with a swastika and signed 'Loki 7,' the letter ended with the salutation "Heil Thor." Police knew that Loki was the Norse God of Mischief but found it no help in tracking down the bomber.

In June of 1996, another letter arrived at the desk of Marlene Stanton of the CBC, warning of a bomb set among the tanks of a Speedy Propane compound. Police found the device and detonated it safely. In all, Loki 7 wrote seven letters over a period of thirteen months before he was caught.

In 1997, Roger Charles Bell, a chemistry teacher from Murray Harbour, was arrested and charged in connection with the bombings. He pleaded guilty to all three bombings and also one that occurred at Nova Scotia's Point Pleasant Park in 1994. He was sentenced to ten years in prison. He has never revealed the motive behind the bombings.

Did you know...

. . . that PEI Crime Stoppers was incorporated as a registered charity in 1988 and started operation on January 4, 1989? As of 2014, they have solved 1,125 cases and have recovered/ seized property and drugs valued at $2,806,432.

Weblinks

Statistics Canada

www40.statcan.ca/l01/cst01/legal04a.htm

If you are interested in how PEI rates of crime stack up against those of Canada's other provinces, these statistics from Stats Canada are for you.

Crime Stoppers

www.peicrimestoppers.com

For more on how to prevent crime in PEI, check out this page, maintained by the PEI chapter of Crime Stoppers.

Charlottetown Police Department

www.city.charlottetown.pe.ca/cityhall/police.cfm

Read about policing, city bylaws and everything else police-related in the provincial capital.

Culture

When most people think of PEI's culture, the thing that leaps to mind is Anne of Green Gables. While Anne certainly does cast a long shadow on the Island, the Island's culture is much more diverse. The province's music, art, literature and performing arts celebrate the Island's different cultures. From the Mi'kmaq to les Acadiens, from the Scots to the Lebanese, PEI culture is a fusion of the traditions that is unique.

ARTISTS
- Number of artists in Canada: 140,000
- Number on PEI: 500
- Number of museums on PEI: 47
- Number of art galleries on PEI: 17

Source: Canada Council for the Arts.

THAT'S AN ORDER
- Number of Islanders given the Order of Canada: 69
- Members of the Order: 55
- Officers of the Order: 8
- Companions of the Order: 1

Source: Governor General of Canada.

Take 5 FIVE MOVIES AND/OR TV SHOWS
SET OR PRODUCED ON PEI

1. *Anne of Green Gables* – the famous Montgomery work that put the Island on the map
2. *Emily of New Moon* – a series based on another Montgomery work
3. *Chef at Home and Chef at Large* – hosted by local Chef Michael Smith
4. *Eckhart* – an animated series based on a book by PEI author David Weale
5. *Doodlez* – animated shorts

IN ORDER

The Order of Prince Edward Island gives public recognition to "individual Islanders whose efforts and accomplishments truly have been exemplary." The Insignia of the Order of Prince Edward Island includes an enameled medallion – the Medal of Merit, which incorporates the provincial emblem against a background of gold and blue, a stylized lapel pin and a miniature medal for less formal occasions. The Medal of Merit is worn with a ribbon of rust, green and white. Recipients of the Order also receive an official certificate and are entitled to use the letters OPEI after their names.

RECOGNITION FOR THE ARTS

In 2012-13, the Canada Council for the Arts provided $287,315 worth of funding to the arts on PEI. In addition to the initial funding, $36,421 was paid to 78 authors through the Public Lending Right

Did you know...

. . . that a 2002 Hyundai Sonata commercial was filmed on the Confederation Bridge? Filming was limited to five-minute periods near sunrise and sunset to allow bridge traffic to keep moving.

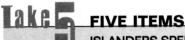

FIVE ITEMS

ISLANDERS SPEND THEIR CULTURAL DOLLARS ON (PER CAPITA)

1. **Newspapers** ($49)
2. **Books** ($24)
3. **Live performing arts** ($20)
4. **Magazines and periodicals** ($18)
5. **Live sports events** ($15)

Commission, bringing to the Island $323,736 in grants. Disciplines receiving money included media arts, music, theatre, visual arts and writing and publishing, with the lion's share of $150,700 going to visual arts. Second in the receiving line was media arts, receiving $59,340, with music coming in third with $32,400. An overwhelming cut of the funding, 92.50 percent, went to artists and organizations in Charlottetown.

In 2012-13, Prince Edward Island artists and organizations received 0.20 percent of Canada Council funding to artists, while PEI includes 0.34% of all Canadian artists.

Source: Canada Council for the Arts.

FILM

Though only two movies have been filmed on the Island in recent years — *The Ballad of Jack and Rose*, a screenplay by Rebecca Miller and *Ghost Cat*, a 2003 animal planet television film starring Ellen Page— there are a number of TV projects on the go each year. In 2000, the industry spent $15.7 million through 18 projects, and $9 million through 31 projects in 2005. In 2015 a third was under production on PEI. *Lucy Maud Montgomery's Anne of Green Gables* will be released in 2016.

• Number of movie theatres on PEI: 5

- Average amount that PEI households spent in movie theatres: $99.00
- Number of drive-in theatres on PEI: 2
- Annual per-capita attendance at theatres and drive-ins on PEI: 4.1

Source: InfoPEI; Statistics Canada

The Little Girl from Cavendish

Born in Clifton, PEI (near present-day New London) in 1874, Lucy Maud Montgomery's influence has been felt across the whole Island and a multitude of industries, such as tourism, film and retail. Every single Islander knows well Montgomery's fictional character, Anne of Green Gables.

Montgomery's literary successes belied an extraordinarily humble upbringing. Before her second birthday Montgomery's mother died. Her widower father moved out west, and she went to live with her maternal grandparents in Cavendish. Being the only child on a homestead owned and operated by an elderly couple - and with few friends nearby - Montgomery had to depend on her imagination and the world around her for companionship and amusement.

Montgomery flourished in school. It was the outlet she needed, and she eventually became an educator herself. Montgomery taught for a few years before moving to Halifax where she was one of only a few women students at Dalhousie University. After earning a degree in English Literature, she taught school on PEI until the 1898 death of her grandfather. At that point she returned to Cavendish to care for her grandmother. Thirteen years later her grandmother's death freed Montgomery to marry her secret fiancé of five years, the Reverend Ewan Macdonald.

Following marriage, Montgomery moved to Ontario, and never

MUSEUMS

- Number of community museums: 33
- Number of provincial museums: 8
- Number of federal museums: 6

Source: Info PEI - Arts, Culture and Heritage.

again returned to live on PEI. In spirit, however, she never left. Nineteen of her twenty novels and most of her short stories are set on the Island. While Montgomery's work is extensive and varied, her most famous work is, of course, Anne of Green Gables.

And then comes Anne

Written in 1905, Montgomery's first novel drew on her own experiences as a lonely child being raised, motherless, by an elderly couple. The book depicts orphaned Anne Shirley, a redheaded, freckled, excessively chatty and wildly imaginative girl sent to live with the Cuthberts, a bachelor and his spinster sister.

Anne of Green Gables almost didn't happen. Disheartened by many rejections, Montgomery put the manuscript away for two years before deciding to try one more time. Boston-based Page Company picked up the book, immediately turning it into a bestseller and a stepping-stone for Montgomery's career. By 1917, though, her relationship with the U.S. publisher had soured and she signed with Canadian publishing powerhouse McClelland and Stewart and American publisher Frederick Stokes.

Montgomery died in Ontario in 1942 and, in death, returned to her beloved Island home. Lucy Maud Montgomery is interred in the Cavendish cemetery.

CONFED CENTRE

Well-known Canadian architect, Dimitri Dimakopoulos, and theatre designer and theorist, George Izenour, teamed up to design the Centre in 1964. The complex covers a city block, can seat nearly 1,100 and is the most important physical institution in the province.

While funding has been sporadic since its inception, the building does mark the first time in Canadian history that every province in the country funded something outside their borders. The project was

Take 5 FIVE PHENOMENA THAT HAVE TURNED CHARLOTTETOWN INTO A "COSMOPOLITAN" CITY

1. **PEI Jazz and Blues Festival:** Founded in 2005, this festival turns downtown Charlottetown into a mecca of jazz and blues for one week in July.

2. **Victoria Row:** Richmond Street in Charlottetown, alongside the Confederation Centre, is blocked off to traffic in the summer and features sidewalk cafes, trendy boutiques and galleries, and free live jazz every day. On Victoria Row, you can hang out, write, e-mail and people watch.

3. **42nd Street & Churchill's:** 42nd Street is a New York-style bar with excellent martinis and single malts; Churchill's is the closest thing to a British/Irish pub. Both are relaxed, unpretentious places where one is likely to encounter the town's intelligentsia, lumpen culturati and other jolly riff-raff.

4. **Arts Guild:** A renovated performance space, across from the Confederation Centre, for local theatre and musicians.

5. **Asian and South Asian food:** A half-dozen restaurants and tea houses have appeared featuring Indian buffets, Thai food based on Buddhist principles and other Asian cuisine. These add to the excellent established Lebanese eateries.

meant to be a functional memorial to the country's Founding Fathers, and is heralded as a place where the nation's culture and multicultural traditions are displayed and celebrated.

Take 5   ACTRESS TOBY TARNOW'S FIVE BEST THINGS ABOUT PLAYING ANNE OF GREEN GABLES

Toby Tarnow first encountered *Anne of Green Gables* at eight when she read the book and selected several pages to perform for a CBC Radio audition.

Tarnow recalls that playing the original Anne in the musical was a dream come true. Recently, Tarnow brought the magic of Anne to an American audience. In 2006, she directed the musical for the Amato Center Theater in Milford, New Hampshire.

1. Visiting PEI, the magical Island, for a reunion in 2005 with Elaine Campbell and Don Harron, the writers of the musical, and visiting the scenes of L.M. Montgomery's story in person.

2. Playing Anne in the CBC radio series for two seasons when I was 14 and 15.

3. Being chosen as the very first Anne in the original CBC TV production of the musical when I was 18.

4. Singing and dancing in the musical and having red hair to match my own freckles!

5. Directing *Anne of Green Gables* the musical in October 2006, the 50th anniversary of the original production, for the Riverbend Youth Company, a program of the Souhegan Valley Boys and Girls Club, with Elaine Campbell and Don Harron attending the opening night.

ARTS SPENDING

- Total amount Islanders spend on cultural goods and services: $100,000,000
- The per capita average annual spending on the arts on PEI: $767

Bio MILTON ACORN

Milton James Edward Acorn was born in Charlottetown in 1923. It is not unusual for poets to try and string together a livelihood while publishing poetry and Acorn was no different. He didn't come from money, so he worked as a fireman, freight handler, longshoreman and carpenter.

After serving in World War II, Acorn moved to Montreal. It was there in 1956 that he published his first poetry collection, *In Love and Anger*. In Montreal Acorn found himself part of a 'who's who' of Canadian poetry, creating alongside the likes of Al Purdy, Irving Layton, Louis Dudek and Frank Scott.

Acorn was an enigma to even those who knew him well. He no sooner was established in Montreal, when he moved to Toronto. Taking his poetry to the city's coffee houses, he earned the reputation as being the "Trubador of the working class," as the magazine *Quill and Quire* put it.

His literary stature continued to grow. As in Montreal, Acorn was part of a group of important poets including Margaret Atwood, David Donnell, Dennis Lee, George Miller and Joe Rosenblatt. It was here he also met poet Gwendolyn MacEwen, whom he married in 1962. When their marriage ended, Acorn

They Said It

"You could go for years without seeing him, and yet he'll always be there somehow, a great craggy presence at the back of your mind, a gnarled tree in silhouette on the horizon."

– Poet Gwendolyn MacEwen, of Milton Acorn, her one-time husband.

moved on again, this time to Vancouver.

On the west coast he published *Jawbreakers*. In Vancouver, he also help found the *The Georgia Strait*, an alternative newspaper still published today.

In 1969, Acorn returned to Toronto, where he published his highly-regarded *I've Tasted My Blood*, a collection which earned him a Canadian Poet's award. In 1972 he published *More Poems For People* followed quickly by *The Island Means Minago* (1975), which won the Governor General's Award.

By 1981, Acorn was to make his final move, this time back to where it all began in Charlottetown. Although his health was in decline, Acorn continued to write and publish during his years on the Island. In 1982, Ragwood Press published *Captain Neal MacDougal & the Naked Goddess*. Four years later, on August 20, 1986, Milton Acorn died.

Acorn's poetry, however, lives on. Like many poets, he is much more widely read and respected today than he was during his lifetime. Next to Lucy Maud Montgomery, he is the most important Island literary figure.

They Said It

ON PEI, THE AVERAGE DOLLARS SPENT ON (PER CAPITA/TOTAL SPENT):

- Home entertainment: $350/$48 million
- Reading material: $128/$17 million
- Photographic equipment and services: $65/$9 million
- Art works and events: $43/$6 million
- Movie theatre admissions: $38/$5 million
- Art supplies and musical instruments: $28/$4 million

Source: Canada Council for the Arts.

LITERATURE

- Total revenue of the book selling industry on PEI: $1.475 million
- Amount Islanders spend on books each year: $3.3 million
- Number of members in the PEI Writers Guild: Over 70

Did you know...

. . . that more than 250,000 people from all over the world visit PEI's Green Gables site each year?

Did you know...

. . . that *Anne of Green Gables* has been translated into seventeen languages and continues to be a favorite around the globe, particularly in Japan where it became part of the school curriculum in 1952?

They Said It

" *[The Fathers of Confederation Memorial Building]* is a tribute to those famous men who founded our Confederation. But it is also dedicating to the fostering of those things that enrich the mind and delight the heart, those intangible things that give meaning to a society and help create from it a civilization and a culture."

– Prime Minister L.B. Pearson, opening ceremonies for the Confederation Centre of the Arts, 1964

 WRITER AND PROFESSOR RICHARD LEMM'S
LIST OF THE FIVE MOST ESTABLISHED PEI POETS (WITH THREE OR MORE PUBLISHED BOOKS)

Richard Lemm is a professor of creative writing and Canadian and post-colonial literature at the University of Prince Edward Island, and a former president of the League of Canadian Poets. He has published four books of poetry and a biography of the Island's most famous poet, *Milton Acorn: In Love and Acorn.* Along with several other Island poets, he sustains the Wordsworth-and-Coleridge tradition of taking long nature walks, but with golf clubs...this is PEI, after all.

1. **David Helwig** (also a prolific fiction writer and essayist)
2. **John Smith**, PEI's first poet laureate
3. **Lesley-Anne Bourne** (also a novelist)
4. **Hugh MacDonald** (also a novelist)
5. **Frank Ledwell**, the Island's former poet laureate.

Broad Strokes

At the turn of the last century, Robert Harris was the most renowned portrait painter in Canada. At his death, Harris had completed about 300 portraits of Canada's most important business, social and political personalities.

Born in Wales, Harris moved to PEI with his family at age seven. As a youngster, Harris was preoccupied with drawing, demonstrating a talent his mother immediately recognized and nurtured. She supported his skill and his eventual relocation to Liverpool. He then spent two years in Boston, studying and working as a novice painter on portraits – some commissioned from photos of the speakers of PEI's House of Assembly – saving enough money to return to Europe.

Between 1876 and 1882, Harris spent time in England, Paris, Rome, PEI and Toronto, building his reputation as an artist and a portrait painter. From 1893 until 1906, he served as president of the Royal Canadian Academy of the Arts and taught at the Ontario School of Art.

In 1883, Harris began work on what would become his most famous piece, a painting entitled "The Fathers of Confederation," portraying the 1864 Quebec meeting of British North America delegates to discuss union. Using photographs and information gathered from the delegates and their families, Harris set to work on the finest canvas money could buy. Completed a year later, the work was displayed in the centre block of the Parliament buildings, where it stayed until a 1916 fire destroyed the block and the painting.

Harris was asked to recreate the painting but he refused citing a busy schedule and poor health. He suggested the government purchase the original sketch from which he made the final painting. That sketch is currently housed in the National Gallery of Canada. Harris died in 1919. In 1928 his widow commissioned the Robert Harris Memorial Gallery and Library in Charlottetown, which became part of the Confederation Centre.

Take 5 FIVE CURRENT BEST-SELLING
AUTHORS AND POETS WHO LIVE ON PEI

1. David Weale
2. David Helwig
3. John MacKenzie
4. Michael Hennessey
5. Anne Compton

DINING

- Number of restaurants, bars and caterers in the province: 370
- Number of people they employ: 5,700
- Industry sales in 2014: $252 million
- Industry's share of provincial GDP: 5.0 percent

Source: Canadian Restaurant and Foodservices Association.

CHARLOTTETOWN FARMERS MARKET

Looking for something to do on a Saturday morning? Look no further if you're close to the capital city. Spend a leisurely morning shopping and eating at the Charlottetown Farmer's Market, located across the street from UPEI. There, you'll find more prepared food than you can imagine, from samosas and fried eggs to smoked salmon and crusty

Did you know...

. . . that with 40 artists in a work force of just under 1,100, Lot 65 near Charlottetown boasts the highest level of artists in Atlantic Canada?

Did you know...

. . . that the Victoria Playhouse, located in the tiny community of Victoria by the Sea (population of approximately 150), presents an average of eighty-five performances a year? During the peak season, the Playhouse operates seven days a week.

European baguettes. The market is open year-round on Saturday mornings, and Wednesday mornings during the summer.

CHEERS

PEI's annual Wine Festival was first celebrated in 1994. Prominent at the show are the offerings of Rossignol Estates, the Island's first and only winery. Rossignol has done well since its inception: the winery took first place for Pinot Noir and Strawberry-Rhubarb in the 1997

Take 5 FIVE FAMOUS PEOPLE
WHO LIVE OR VACATION ON PEI

With its picturesque landscape, fresh island breezes and reputation for hospitality, it's no wonder that PEI is home, at least part of the time, to these and other famous faces:

1. **Lorne Elliott** – prominent Canadian comedian of CBC Radio's "Madly Off in All Directions" fame.

2. **Brad Richards** – born and raised on the Island, this Stanley Cup winning NHL star and Olympian is PEI's "favorite son."

3. **Colleen Dewhurst and George C. Scott** – this famous Hollywood couple used to own a summer home in Bay Fortune. The home has since been converted into The Inn, widely considered one of the Island's best restaurants.

4. **The Campbells** – Canadian theatre elite Norman and Elaine Campbell had a home on the Island for years. Norman, who passed away in 2004, helped turn *Anne of Green Gables* into a musical and annual production.

5. **Chef Michael Smith** – star of the hit cooking shows "The Inn Chef" and "Chef at Home."

Did you know...

. . . that Islander Brad Richards was named the Canadian Hockey League Player of the Year in 1999-2000?

Nova Scotia Taster's Choice Awards and, that same year, won two silver medals from the International Wine Competition in New York for its Seyval Blanc and Marechal Foch. Thanks to its nine acres – seven planted outside and two in greenhouses – Rossignol boasts a 45,000 bottle-capacity and a wide range of fruit and table wines.

Take 5 TOP FIVE GOLD CUP AND SAUCER STRETCH DRIVES

1. **2003 Sand Olls Dexter** - nipped Harmony P in a furious come-from-behind effort to thwart Mike MacDonald's attempt at a record six Gold Cup victories.

2. **1986 Rev Your Engine** - emerged victorious after a dramatic stretch duel with Maritime-bred Angel's Shadow over a sloppy track.

3. **2002 London Mews N** - after posting the fastest half-mile in Maritime racing history, driver Gilles Barrieau managed to hold off hard closing R J's Dexter by a nose.

4. **1973 Dr. Walter C** - the only Island-bred winner prevailed in a close summary over heavy favorite Gons Butler in the last of the two-heat Gold Cup finals.

5. **1983 Silent Class** - Marcel Barrieau piloted this underdog in a battle of Moncton-owned horses defeating Autopilot.

Take 5 — FIVE FAMOUS LOBSTER SUPPERS ON PEI

1. **New Glasgow Lobster Supper:** "Home of the Original PEI Lobster Supper" – New Glasgow, since 1958.
2. **St. Ann's Parish** – one of the "World's Famous Lobster Suppers" – Hope River, since 1963.
3. **Fisherman's Wharf Lobster Supper** – "Largest and Most Modern on PEI" – North Rustico, since 1980.
4. **Lobster on the Wharf** – "The Place for Lobster" – Charlottetown, since 1981.
5. **Cardigan Lobster Suppers** – "Eastern PEI's Original" – Cardigan, since 1976.

PROFESSIONAL SPORTS

PEI has just one professional sports team. Charlottetown is home base to the Quebec Major Junior Hockey League's PEI Rocket.

NAGANO GOLD

In 1967, an Olympian was born in Charlottetown. David "Eli" MacEachern would leave his mark on the sport of bobsledding in Canada and on the world stage.

In 1994, breakman MacEachern and his partner Peirre Lueders jettisoned to the top of the Nagano Olympic podium, making history on the way. The cumulative time of MacEachern's and Lueder's Olympic four bobsleigh heats was 3:37.24. This score was a great one and placed them in first. It was, however, the exact same score earned by the Italian team. And so, for the first time in Olympic bobsledding history, two teams shared the gold medal.

Did you know...

. . . that famous singers Tom Petty and Kris Kristofferson are rumoured to vacation on PEI?

They Said It

"*People in Japan have long held a keen interest in Prince Edward Island so anything that's actually a bona fide Island product is of interest to the Japanese people.*"

– Island winery owner, John Rossignol.

Olympic glory aside, MacEachern's career has been extraordinary. He boasts 28 World Cup medals, five World Cup titles and a world championship silver medal. After nine years on Canada's National Bobsled team, David retired from racing. He now owns Dynamic Fitness Incorporated in Charlottetown, a training and consultative business that helps professional athletes.

GOLD CUP AND SAUCER

Two of the most famous PEI cultural events are the Gold Cup and Saucer Parade and the Gold Cup and Saucer Race. Islanders and visitors alike have enjoyed these events every August since 1961. Back in 1960, after the first Gold Cup and Saucer horse race at the Charlottetown Driving Park Entertainment Centre, two visionaries conspired to ensure that many more folks would enjoy the race the following year.

The Park's 'Duck' Acorn and local journalist Bill Hancox thought a beauty pageant, won by the girl whose horse won the race, would draw in the crowds and if it didn't, a parade planned around the race certainly would. The Gold Cup and Saucer Parade is still held in Charlottetown every year the day before the race, kicking off Old

They Said It

"*I'm going to the Olympics.*"

— The prophetic words of Olympic gold medallist, Islander Dave MacEachern, as written in 1986 in his high school yearbook.

Home Week – the Island's pre-eminent agricultural event. For a dramatic start to the race, the arena is darkened - save for one spotlight into which each horse and rider enters to be introduced to the crowd. Once that's finished, it's straight to 'on your marks.' Some of the fastest horses and riders from all over the region ride the racetrack lines for nine days in this prestigious event, all eyeing the $60,000 pot.

Source: Charlottetown Driving Park and Entertainment Centre.

RAINBOW VALLEY

The summer of 2005 marked the end of an era on PEI. On Labour Day of that year, the beloved amusement park, Rainbow Valley, closed its trademark rainbow gate for the last time. Sprawling across 40 acres, Rainbow Valley had it all. From water slides to paddle boats, from a petting zoo to the famous Flying Saucer gift shop, visitors returned year after year. Rainbow Valley made indelible mark on Islanders and tourists of all ages.

They Said It

"*We would like Parks Canada to reconsider their decision to close Rainbow Valley at the end of the Summer of 2005 and consider putting the money into maintaining Rainbow Valley and upgrading it for future generations to come.*"

– Petition protesting the closure of Rainbow Valley

Take 5 TOP FIVE NON-MUSIC FESTIVALS
ON THE ISLAND

1. **Charlottetown Festival**
2. **Potato Blossom Festival**
3. **Old Home Week**
4. **PEI International Shellfish Festival**
5. **PEI Studios Tour Weekend**

LET THERE BE LIGHT

Now touted as the largest Canada Day festival east of Ottawa, the Atlantic Superstore-sponsored Festival of Lights in Charlottetown is the place to be on July 1st. After all, where better to celebrate Canada's birthday than in the Cradle of Confederation?

The annual festival is a four-day event that offers summertime fun for everyone. The event offers typical festival requisites such as beer gardens and Buskers, but also includes sand sculpting demonstrations, extreme trampoline shows and rock-climbing walls.

The main draws, however, are the popular musical acts that draw crowds from the Island, the mainland and beyond. Recent festivals have boasted such acts as The Tragically Hip and 3 Doors Down.

The third main component of the festival is the elaborate fireworks show held in celebration of Canada Day. The largest pyrotechnic display in Atlantic Canada, the festival's fireworks show has been timed as one of the longest in the country.

A festival of this magnitude doesn't come without cost, but it is money well spent as it generates millions for the province.

Did you know...

. . . that golf generates an estimated $147 million for the PEI economy, with almost 80 percent of that total being non-golfing consumption?

Source: National Allied Golf Association 2014

GOLF PEI

Back in 1989, a group of six golf course operators had the foresight to realize that to grow their own business, they needed to grow the golf industry on PEI. They also recognized that they needed to work together to maximize the effect of their efforts. To do that, they formed Golf PEI, an industry association devoted to the promotion and development of golf on PEI.

To achieve the success it's enjoyed, PEI's golf industry has made a commitment to develop the game, the product (as the operators like to call their courses) and the public's awareness. This dedication has paid off. Recently ten of PEI's golf courses were rated among the top 100 courses in Canada, as per *The Globe and Mail's* golf publication, '*Globe Golf.*' Holland College's Canadian Golf Academy, located in Stratford, welcomes golfers of all ages and skill levels. CPGA certified instructors teach group and individual lessons using state-of-the-art equipment.

Did you know...

. . . that Pro golfers such as Tom Watson, Mike Weir, John Daly, Fred Couples and Jack Nicklaus have all tested their skills at some of PEI's courses?

Weblinks

The Confederation Centre of the Arts

www.confederationcentre.com

This home page of the Confederation Centre of the Arts is complete with listings of coming events and all things cultural.

L.M. Montgomery Institute

www.lmmontgomery.ca/lmmi

Affiliated with the University of Prince Edward Island, the Institute offers information on the writer and her legacy, as well as up-to-date events and products that promote her many works.

PEI Arts Council

www.peiartscouncil.com

This site is a must for anyone interested in the Island's arts and artists.

Gallery Listing

www.gov.pe.ca/infopei/index.php3?number=66481&lang=e

Interested in visiting PEI galleries? This comprehensive listing tells you where to look for art galleries on the Island, with weblinks to each gallery.

National Historic Monuments

www.gov.pe.ca/infopei/index.php3?number=59339&lang=E

Want to see where arts history was made on PEI? This website offers a comprehensive list of National Historic Monuments found throughout the Island.

Festivals PEI

www.festivalspei.com

For information on the festivals that dot the Island throughout the year, this is where it's at.

Economy

Prince Edward Island has an increasingly diversifying economy. A strong agricultural and tourism base has been complemented by a growing manufacturing and high tech sector, including a vibrant aerospace industry. It has a highly educated workforce and competitive taxes have a made it a desirable place to do business.

GROSS DOMESTIC PRODUCT
(TOTAL VALUE OF GOODS/SERVICES)
In 2014, PEI's GDP was valued at $4.644 billion.
- Per capita GDP: $39,780
- GDP growth in 2014: 1.3 percent over 2013

INCOME
- Median family income on PEI: $69,010
- Median Canadian family income: $75.540
- Median family income in Newfoundland and Labrador: $70,900
- Median family income in New Brunswick: $65,910
- Median family income in Nunavut: $65,530

Source: Statistics Canada.

Take 5   TOP FIVE EXPENSES

OF PEI HOUSEHOLDS

1. **Shelter** 28.8%
2. **Income Tax** 25%
3. **Transportation** 20.6%
4. **Food** 13.6%
5. **Insurance and pension contributions** 10%

Source: Statistics Canada.

INCOME CHANGES

PEI incomes have increased each year between 2010 and 2014. In 2010, individual Islanders earned an average $706.56 a week; by 2014, this had grown to $773.83. By way of comparison, Canadians as a whole earned an average of $935.31 a week in 2014, with the highest wages being in the Northwest Territories ($1,381.37).

BY THE HOUR

As of January 2014, Islanders over the age of 15 earned an average hourly salary of $20.82. Men garnered an average $21.17 and women, $20.82. Unionized workers averaged $26.95 an hour, while non-unionized workers pulled in $17.67. As of October 2014, minimum wage on the Island is $10.20.

Source: Statistics Canada and Government of Prince Edward Island.

DEBT

Collectively, Islanders owe $ 2.120 billion. Just over 66 percent of that debt comes in the form of mortgages, while 11 percent is owed on vehicle loans. About 5.4 percent of the total owing can be chalked up to credit card debt.

Islanders are in debt, on average, to the tune of $33,569. That compares to Canadians on the whole being in the hole an average of $55,200.

Source: Statistics Canada.

Anne of Green(back) Gables

Anne of Green Gables may have been the fictional invention of Lucy Maud Montgomery, but the money she generates is very real. The rambunctious redhead has become one of the Island's greatest commodities and continues to bring great riches to the province.

First published in 1908, Lucy Maud Montgomery's *Anne of Green Gables* was an instant hit. By 1919, more than 300,000 copies had been sold, and by 1947 sales reached 900,000. By 2014, 50 million copies had sold, 45 versions of the novel were in print, along with a plethora of Anne-related books, such as diaries and cookbooks and it had been translated into 20 languages.

Despite its phenomenal success, however, Montgomery herself earned only a modest sum from her famous book. In contrast, PEI has reaped much reward from her masterpiece and the beloved 'Anne.' Each year, an average 700,000 people visit the Island. Of these, approximately 120,000 visit Province House in Charlottetown, the 1864 "birthplace" of Canadian Confederation, while three times as many visit Cavendish, the fictitious birthplace of Anne Shirley.

For decades, Montgomery's descendants received no royalties for her works as it was believed that the original publisher of *Anne of Green Gables*, L.C. Page Co., held all copyrights. In 1985, however, it was discovered that this was simply not the case.

In 1928, Montgomery signed an agreement with the company that reverted copyright back to her estate and heirs upon her death. In 1994, the Anne of Green Gables Licensing Authority was established to regulate the vast array of Anne-inspired souvenirs. Royalties for 'Anne' products are now divided between the province and Montgomery's heirs.

A stroll through any Island gift shop proves that anything 'Anne' sells. There are 110 companies licensed to use the image or name of Anne Shirley on virtually anything: dolls, girl-sized wigs with the familiar red braids, plates, ashtrays, fridge magnets, wristwatches, buttons, calendars, mouse pads, tea, preserves, potting soil, seeds, maple syrup, tea sets, prints and posters, rugs, curtains, pins, hair accessories, lollipops, Christmas balls, puzzles, furniture, aprons, sculptures, house signs, stained-glass windows, soap, cookies, chocolates and potato chips.

TAXES

- Provincial sales tax: 9 percent
- Combined provincial sales tax and federal GST (HST): 5 percent + 9 percent
- Average tax rate (includes all forms of taxes) for Island families in 2013: 24.8-45.7 percent
- Average personal income tax paid by Islanders: $7196
- Corporate tax rate: 4.5 percent

Source: Government of Prince Edward Island; Canada Customs and Revenue Agency.

Spud Island

The potato is quite literally the root of PEI society and economy. No one can put an exact date on when the potato was first introduced but it was sometime after the French were deported from the colony in 1758 and before 1771, the year that the governor of the colony reported the crop to be a "phenomenal success."

Early potato planting was not easy. Settlers had to fell the dense forests that covered the Island and plant their crops between tree stumps that could not be budged. Nevertheless, potato farms prospered thanks to the Island's fertile, acidic soil. By 1830, potatoes were PEI's main export. In the 1840s, PEI fields were hard hit by the same blight that caused the Irish famine, but the industry recovered.

In the 1920s, the creation of modern processing technologies and the introduction of two new varieties, the Irish Cobbler and the Green Mountain, saw the birth of the modern PEI potato industry.

The 1950s saw massive changes to industry across North America and the PEI potato industry was no different. Potato farming faced profound re-orientation as small family-owned farms gave way to larger, more mechanized farm operations. This resulted in fewer

TAX FREEDOM DAY

Tax freedom day (day on which earnings no longer go to taxes (2010) is June 6 nationally).

- Alberta: May 16
- New Brunswick: May 31
- Ontario: June 1
- **Prince Edward Island: June 3**
- Manitoba: June 7
- British Columbia: June 8
- Nova Scotia: June 11

Islanders actually farming potatoes. In 1940, nearly 11,000 Islanders grew potatoes, but by 1965 that number had dropped to 6,500 farmers and to only 550 by 2002. Fewer farmers, however, did not result in fewer potatoes. In 1940, farmers grew 37,000 acres, in 1965, 44,000 acres and by 1990, more than 75,000 acres were dedicated to potatoes.

Between 1987 and 1990, Island potato fields were afflicted by the PYVN virus and this led the USA and other markets to close their borders to PEI seed potatoes. In 2000, the discovery of potato wart in a PEI field had a similar effect, and borders were again closed until scientists proved the case was isolated.

Nevertheless, the Island's potato industry has survived. In 2014, the harvest generated $ 1billion for the PEI economy. It seems that Canadians and Islanders still have a love affair with the almighty potato. Canadians eat, on average, 72.67 kg of fresh and processed potatoes per capita.

Island farmers grow 25% of all Canadian potatoes. They also export potato and potato products to over 20 countries — 20 percent go to the United States.

- Quebec June 12
- Newfoundland and Labrador: June 16
- Saskatchewan: June 20

Source: The Fraser Institute.

GOVERNMENT EXPENDITURE: HOW PEI SPENDS ITS CASH

- Percentage spent on health/social services: 36%
- Education: 14%
- Debt service: 12%
- Transportation and communication: 6%
- Community Services and Seniors: 6%
- Advanced Learning: 8%
- Finance, Justice and Environment: 13%
- Natural Resources 5%

Source: Statistics Canada.

GOVERNMENT DEBT

Deficit for fiscal year 2014	$39.6 million
Provincial debt as of 2014	$2.117 billion
Increase that is since 2102-13:	16%
Debt as percentage of GDP	36.2 percent

Source: Government of PEI, Statistics Canada; Greater Charlottetown Area Chamber of Commerce.

INFLATION

In 2014, the inflation rate on PEI stood at 1.6 percent. In comparison, the national rate of inflation that year was 1.1 percent.

Source: Statistics Canada.

EMPLOYMENT (2015)

Labour force 84,700

Employed 74,000

Unemployed 10,700

Unemployment rate 11.5 percent

Source: Statistics Canada.

Flexing Some Mussel

Between 1980 and today, Island cultured mussel landings grew from 40 tonnes to more than 18,000 tonnes and an industry worth more than $23 million. The industry creates direct and indirect jobs for 2,500 Islanders. PEI mussels are renowned across North America for their taste and quality and PEI accounts for more than 80 percent of the mussels consumed by North Americans.

PEI's mussel industry, which is based in estuaries on the Island's eastern and northern shores, uses what is known as a long-line system. Mussels are hung in "socks" placed on long ropes that are suspended in the water.

Mussels grow on these lines for 18-24 months before they are harvested. During winter months, mussel lines are sunk below the ice cover. Those lines that come to maturity and must be harvested in winter months require harvesters to cut holes in the ice. Scuba divers then enter frigid waters and free lines from their moorings. At other times of the year, mussel lines are drawn in by boats.

Once harvested, mussels are processed in one of PEI's eight federally and provincially licensed processing plants. The mussels are separated, washed and have their "beards" removed before they are inspected and packaged for sale to markets across North America.

Take 5 — TOP FIVE GDP-GENERATING INDUSTRIES ON PEI
(PERCENT OF GDP)

1. **Tourism**
2. **Manufacturing**
3. **Construction**
4. **Agriculture**
5. **Service**

EMPLOYMENT SECTORS

Sectors in which Islanders are employed as of May 2015:

Trade:	10, 600
Healthcare and social assistance :	9,600
Public administration:	7,600
Manufacturing:	6,000 :
Construction:	5,200
Accommodation and food services:	5,500
Educational services:	5, 300
Agriculture:	3,700
Forestry, fishing, mining and oil and gas:	2,600
Information, culture and recreation:	2,300
Other services:	3,300
Transportation and warehousing:	2,800
Business, building and other support services:	2,100
Professional, scientific and technical services:	2,900
Finance, insurance, real estate and leasing:	2,700
Utilities:	300

Source: Statistics Canada.

PUBLIC ADMINISTRATION

In 2013, 17,656 Islanders worked for government or a government Agency.

- Federal Island employees: 3,746
- Provincial: 8,048
- Local: 882
- Health and Social Services: 9,600
- Education: 5,300

Source: Statistics Canada.

Take 5 TOP FIVE THINGS PADERNO
ENJOYS ABOUT DOING BUSINESS ON PEI

Paderno cookware is made in Prince Edward Island and is the only cookware manufacturer in Canada. Since 1979, they have been turning the cookware industry on its ear with their famous Pots for Eternity, which have found a home in thousands of kitchens all over North America, including the residence of Canada's Prime Minister, and the cookware of choice aboard Air Force One. All cookware is made from solid 18/10 stainless steel and comes with a 25-year warranty.

1. **Golf courses.** If you're having a bad work day, a golf course is always just a few minutes away.
2. **No rush hour.** No matter where you live on PEI, it's never more than a 15 minute drive to work.
3. **Fields of green.** When you daydream outside your office window, all you can see is green, green grass for miles.
4. **Gold Cup Day.** Imagine a whole town shutting down and a day off work for a parade.
5. **Potatoes.** With all those potatoes, somebody's going to need pots to cook them in.

GENDER GAP

Labour force participation rate for women in 2014: 65.7 percent, the second highest in the country

- For men: 73.2
- Island women earn 93.8 percent of what men earn
- Average hourly wage of Island women in 2014: $20.82
- Men: $21.17

Source: Statistics Canada.

Bio THOMAS HALL

Born in Wilmot, PEI in 1836, Thomas Hall was a mechanic and master of wood and iron. He developed a machine shop where he began a small agricultural machinery business. He soon expanded his business, building a modern steam-powered, three-story factory near Summerside. The crux of his agricultural innovations rested in his creation of a threshing machine. He traveled to exhibitions on and off the Island to demonstrate his machinery. In 1881, his thresher won first prize at the Dominion Exhibition in Halifax. The significance of this award helped him sell 45 machines and 50 fanning-mills that year.

Hall's business, by 1884 known as the Hall Manufacturing Company, grew and supplied the growing Island farm economy. Unlike his national competitors, however, Hall never sought patents for any of his innovations and while business thrived on the Island, he never made inroads into further markets in Canada.

When Hall died in 1919, his company was renamed and reorganized. The Hall Manufacturing and Cold Storage Company produced the threshers invented by its founder well into the 1950s.

TOP FIVE GDP-GENERATING SERVICE SECTORS ON PEI
(PERCENT OF GDP)

1. **Finance, insurance, real estate, renting, leasing and company management** (19.7 percent)
2. **Public administration** (12.2 percent)
3. **Health care and social assistance** (9.1 percent)
4. **Retail trade** (7.5 percent)
5. **Educational services** (6 percent)

SHARING THE WEALTH

Islanders donated $28,870,000 to charity. The median amount they donated was $360, $110 more than the national median of $250.

Source: Statistics Canada.

HOW WE GET TO WORK

- 81.9 percent of Islanders drive their own vehicles
- 9.6 percent carpool
- 6.4 percent walk
- 1.9 percent use other means
- 0.02 percent use public transportation

Source: Statistics Canada.

Did you know...

. . . that each year PEI produces over 75 pounds of potatoes per every Canadian?

Did you know...

. . . that there are almost three times as many chickens as people living on PEI?

Take 5 — TOP FIVE LIVESTOCK RAISED

1. **Chickens** (447,061)
2. **Pigs** (123,192)
3. **Cattle, dairy and beef** (86,435)
4. **Sheep** (3,901)
5. **Horses and ponies** (registered) (1,921)

Source: Government of PEI.

ISLAND BUSINESS

- Just over 70 percent of the Island's businesses employ fewer than five people.
- 16 percent have 5-19 employees
- 5.3 percent have 20-49 employees
- 4.8 percent have 50-499 employees
- 3.5 percent have more than 500 employees
- About 66 percent of all workers are employed by small- or medium-sized businesses
- Increase in bankruptcy rate in 2104: 13% over 2013 (the biggest rise of any province)
- Survival rate for SME's in most sectors: 50%

Source: Statistics Canada; Government of PEI; Canadian Federation of Independent Business (CFIB)

Did you know...

. . . that there are more farmers on PEI than there are anywhere else in Canada? About 5.8 percent of the Island's population live on farms, compared with a national average of only three percent. Also, a higher proportion of PEI land is reserved for farming than in any other province.

Take 5 TOP FIVE ISLAND CROPS
(BY ACREAGE)

1. **Tame hay** (157,405 acres)
2. **Potatoes** (97,637 acres)
3. **Barley** (79,248 acres)
4. **Wheat** (27,872 acres)
5. **Oats** (12,551 acres)

Source: Government of PEI.

COST OF HOUSING

PEI is in the middle of the pack in terms of national housing costs, having the fifth lowest in the country. Newfoundland and Labrador, New Brunswick, Saskatchewan and Manitoba have lower. The Island's housing costs are 62 percent of the national average and just 44 percent of British Columbia's, the highest in the nation.

BUYING A HOUSE

The average resale price of a home in Canada — as of May 2015— is $450,886. Homes on PEI are far more affordable. The average resale price for a home here is $ 167,391, the nation's lowest.

Prince Edward Island	**$167,391**
New Brunswick	$164,736
Nova Scotia	$244,608
Manitoba	$279,429
Newfoundland/Labrador	$278,263
Quebec	$276,937

Did you know...

. . . that despite its diminutive size, the Island produces more than 30 percent of the Canadian potato crop each year?

> "*I think there is a real danger that Anne of Green Gables will become prostituted.*"
>
> **– Tom McMillan, a Tory MP from P.E.I. in 1988, on his belief that Anne of Green Gables was being over-marketed.**

Saskatchewan	$304,356
Ontario	$583,766
Alberta	$405,105
British Columbia	$632,182

Source: Canadian Real Estate Association

PRINCE EDWARD ISLAND PRESERVE COMPANY

When Bruce McNaughton turned 200 lbs of frozen strawberries — the casualties of a failed restaurateur attempt — into 450 bottles of preserves, he inadvertently stumbled upon his calling as proprietor of the PEI Preserve Company. From this accidental beginning in 1985, the PEI Preserve Company based in New Glasgow now sells over 100,000 jars of jams, jellies and preserves each year. The company currently employs over 80 people.

AGRICULTURE

Prince Edward Island is a great place to farm. The Island has a total land area of 1.4 million acres with approximately 594,000 acres cleared for agricultural use. Agriculture is very important to the rural way of life with 3.7 percent of the population living on farms. There are 1500 farms engaged in growing crops and raising livestock on PEI.

Did you know...

. . . that the Island is governed by very strict sign laws? Roadside signs, billboards and portable signage are banned. Some municipalities even restrict what kinds of signs can be erected on private property.

They Said It

> "*It's been a lot of fun for us and hopefully it will be fun for many more years.*"
>
> **– Cow's Ice Cream founder, Scott Linkletter**

> "*It's kind of like one of the things you do now when you go to PEI is you go to see Anne and you eat Cows Ice Cream and you go to the beach.*"
>
> **– Scott Linkletter**

These farms range in size from a few acres to 3,000 acres.

Source: Government of PEI.

ON PEI FARMS IN 2014:

- Number of eggs laid: 3.427 million dozen, 1.675 million consumed locally, 1.752 million exported
- Amount of potatoes harvested: 25 million hundredweight (cwt) of product
- Number of acres of potatoes planted in 2014: 90,500
- Number of acres of wheat, oats and barley: 111.500
- Number of acres of lowbush blueberry crops: 13,000
- Percent of PEI farms with are beef farms:40
- Number of dairy farms on PEI: 180
- Annual milk production: Over 100 million litres

Source: Government of PEI.

TOURISM

Tourism is the second most important industry to PEI's economy. In 2014, the total value of sales in tourism-related services was $380,000,000. There were over 1, 200,000 visitors to the Island. Tourism generated 45.5 million dollars in tax revenue.

Source: Government of PEI, Treasury.

FORE!

PEI has 22 golf courses. Ten of these have recently rated among the top 100 golf courses in Canada. According to GolfPEI.ca, golf generates $100 million for the Island's economy. Of that total, $80 million is spent in non-golfing facilities such as restaurants and hotels.

Source: Golf PEI.

COWS ICE CREAM INC.

Cows Ice Cream began in a single shop in Cavendish in 1983. At that time, Cows sold only ice cream. Responding to positive feedback from customers about employees' uniforms, Cows expanded its offerings in 1985 to include t-shirts and other Cows paraphernalia. Today there are 12 Cows outlets throughout North America — seven on the Island, one in Halifax, one in Whistler, B.C., one in Banff, Alberta, one in Niagara on the Lake, ON, and one in the United States in Park City, Utah.

Did you know...

. . . that one year after completion of the Confederation Bridge, tourism on the Island increased by 50 percent? Many came to see the bridge itself.

Take 5 TOP FIVE PLACES FROM WHICH
ISLAND VISITORS HAIL

1. **Ontario** (19.2 percent)
2. **Nova Scotia** (18.4 percent)
3. **New Brunswick** (14.4 percent)
4. **Quebec** (8.9 percent)
5. **New England states** (4.0 percent)

Source: Government of PEI.

A FISH STORY

The fishery continues to be a profitable industry for the Island. In total contribution to the Island economy, it rates third behind agriculture and tourism.

In 2014, over 115 million pounds of fish were landed, valued at over $139 million. Overall, the fishery accounted for over $278 million of the Island's economy in that year, and employed over 12,000 people.

Source: Government of PEI, Agriculture, Fisheries and Aquaculture.

THE PEI FISHERY BOASTS:

- 4150 commercial fishers
- 3,000 processing plant employees
- 1,261 licensed lobster fishers
- 1,279 licensed mackerel fishers
- 1,300 inshore fishing vessels
- 800 licensed groundfish fishers
- 870 licensed herring fishers

Did you know...

. . . that PEI has two lobster seasons? The first, on the north side of the Island, runs from May 1st until the end of June. The second runs on the south side from mid-August to mid-October.

Take 5 — TOP FIVE MOST VALUABLE
CATCHES (VALUE OF CATCH, 2005)

1. **Lobster** (82,382,000)
2. **Mussels** (26,603,000)
3. **Oysters** (5,844,000)
4. **Herring** (5,121,000)
5. **Snow Crab** (3,475,000)

- 42 provincially licensed and federally registered export plants
- 20 provincially licensed non-export plants
- 17 major shellfish producers
- 5 finfish culture sites

Source: Government of PEI.

LOBSTER

Lobster caught in Atlantic waters is highly favoured as the cadillac of lobster; PEI lobsters account for about 20 percent of those caught in Canada.

There are about 1,200 lobster fishers on the Island and the fruits of their labour – the bulk of which come from the area between North Cape and East Point — kick a lot into the province's coffers, impacting the province's GDP by 78.7 million and creating $20 million in tax revenue.

The average catch per fisher in PEI is 22,000 pounds. The delicious delicacy ranks third on the Island's top ten list of species by weight and first on it for value.

Did you know...

. . . that Islanders pay more for their electricity than just about anyone in Canada? Because the province has little to no source of energy – such as coal or petroleum – the bulk of its juice is imported, via an underwater cable, from neighbouring New Brunswick.

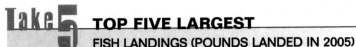

Take 5 TOP FIVE LARGEST
FISH LANDINGS (POUNDS LANDED IN 2005)

1. **Mussels** (35,350,000)
2. **Herring** (33,265,000)
3. **Lobster** (18,485,000)
4. **Marine plants** (13,606,000)
5. **Mackerel** (10,886,000)

MORE LOBSTER

Prior to the 1960s, lobster did not have nearly the prestige that it has today. In fact it was often used as fertilizer on farmers' fields. How times have changed! In 2005, the average price of lobster was $5.58/pound, up 11 percent from the previous year. Compared with 1970, the total value of the lobster haul increased by 1,657 percent, up from $6,231,000 in 1970 to $103,222,000 in 2005. In 2013, the average price was $3.00/pound, the lowest in a long time. In 2014, the average price for market lobster was $4.25/pound. The value of the overall catch was $114,751,810.

Source: Government of PEI, Agriculture, Fisheries and Aquaculture; Government of PEI, Treasury.

TRANSPORTATION INFRASTRUCTURE

- There are 5,648 km of roads on PEI.
- The last railway tracks were torn up in the early 1990s, but remnants of the tracks have been converted to the Confederation Trail, PEI's portion of Canada's national Trans-Canada trail. From tip to tip, the Confederation trail stretches 279 km.

COMMERCIAL FORESTRY

Unlike much of Canada, PEI does not rely heavily on the forest industry nor does the government own much of the province's forests. Approximately 90 percent of the annual harvest takes place on private lands, though the government estimates that harvest to total some 3,000 hectares. The trees, for the most part, end up processed for logs, stud wood, pulp and fuel.

The government also estimates that a third of the province's harvested forest renews itself naturally, another third is converted to other uses — such as agriculture — and about a quarter is planted with commercial species.

Source: Government of PEI — Agriculture, Fisheries and Aquaculture.

BLOWING IN THE WIND

Prince Edward Island is fast becoming a centre of wind energy innovation. The province currently has six wind farms:

- Aeolus Wind Farm, 3 MW
- Eastern Kings Wind Farm, 30 MW
- North Cape Wind Farm, 10.56MW
- Norway Wind Park, 9 MW
- West Cape Wind Park, 99 MW
- Summerside Windfarm, 12 MW

WASTE NOT, WANT NOT

PEI is a leader in recycling — nearly 98 percent of beer and pop bottles are returned for re-use. The Island also has a three-tier waste management system, operated by government-run Island Waste Management Corporation. The program is the only mandatory source separation program in the country.

Did you know...

> . . . that the Island currently gets about five percent of its electricity from wind energy produced at North Cape?

Weblinks

Prince Edward Island Business Women's Association

http://www.peibwa.org

The PEIBWA is a non-profit organization representing businesswomen province-wide. It provides services and programs to help women succeed in the business world.

Prince Edward Island Potato Board

http://www.peipotato.org/

The PEIPB provides information up to date potato industry information to consumers, retailers and potato growers.

Government of Prince Edward Island

http://www.gov.pe.ca

Your online source for all information about Prince Edward Island from the Government of the Province.

Tourism Industry Association of Prince Edward Island

http://www.tiapei.pe.ca

TIAPEI supports programs and projects to assist tourism operators from all sectors and regions of the province.

Did you know...

. . . that Island fishermen harvest almost 30 types of fish and seafood species?

Politics

POLITICS AND PASTURES

Both before and after Europeans settled the Island, there were and are the Mi'kmaq. As one of the seven Mi'kmaq districts that spanned from Newfoundland to eastern Quebec and northern Maine, the Island Mi'kmaq had local chiefs as well as leaders affiliated with the region-wide Mi'kmaq Grand Council.

Europeans brought with them their own political systems. Shortly after the Acadian deportation of 1758, British settler politics on PEI took a definitively Island twist. In 1767, the Island was divided by lottery into 67 lots of 2,000 acres. These tracts were granted to military men and other favoured Britons. In return for grants, landlords were required to pay a rent to the Crown, establish a school and, within ten years, settle at least a third of their land with Protestant settlers.

ABSENTEE LANDLORD

The scheme never worked. Few landlords met the conditions, and farmers who could not own their farmlands came to resent the absentee landlords. They demanded escheat — that Britain purchase the land and offer it free to farmers. Escheators turned to politics to solve the land problem. In 1834, an Escheat Party, led by William Cooper, was elected to the colonial assembly.

They Said It

After several decades of lobbying — and two years after responsible government came to the Island — the colonial government passed a law in 1853 that enabled them to buy lands from willing landlords.

Colonial money dried up, and the law became ineffective. In the 1860s, angry Islanders organized themselves into local Tenant Leagues, united in their resolve to solve the land issue. To compel landlords to sell their land, tenants stopped paying rent. As a rent collector approached, a conch was sounded and farmers would gather in a show of force to impede his progress. Such emotionally charged meetings often ended in violence.

THE BELFAST RIOT

Island politics did not just turn on the land issue. Religious animosity between Catholics and Protestants also fuelled political differences. On March 1, 1847, these two divisive forces in Island politics led to violence at the polls. That day, a by-election was planned in the town of Belfast. The candidates were a landowning Protestant Tory and a Roman Catholic Reformer who supported escheat. Two hundred supporters of both men, armed with bludgeons, descended on Belfast. The result was bloody fisticuffs.

When the dust settled, three men were dead. The election itself was postponed, held another day under military supervision.

Did you know...

. . . that George Coles may be thought of as the "Dueling Premier"? On at least two occasions Coles invited a political opponent to a duel.

JACK MACANDREW'S FIVE

MOST INTERESTING PEI POLITICIANS

Jack MacAndrew has been reporting on, or involved in, PEI politics since 1958 when he covered the election of Premier Walter Shaw for CBC Radio. He was a strategist and speechwriter for Premier Alex Campbell and filled the same role helping elect Premier Joe Ghiz. He owns and operates a promotion, advertising and public relations company called Media Concepts from his century-old farmhouse in Meadow Bank, PEI.

1. **Premier Alex Campbell:** He took office at the age of 33 and dragged Prince Edward Islanders (often kicking and screaming) into the 20th century, revolutionizing the educational system from grade one through university. He was the greatest Islander of the 20th century.

2. **Premier Walter Shaw:** Shaw became premier at the age of 65 after retiring as a career civil servant. A jovial bear of a man, and a great storyteller, Walter Shaw embodied and celebrated the values of his Scottish forbears.

3. **Premier Joe Ghiz:** This son of emigrant Lebanese parents possessed a lightning quick intellect. He learned politics in his father's corner store, and was proud to be the first elected provincial premier of non-European descent in Canada. Islanders, in turn, were immensely proud of him and the key role he played in conferences of provincial premiers.

4. **Allison Ellis:** Ellis was a farmer-fisherman of rock steady principle, who served as cabinet minister in the government of Premier Joe Ghiz. Allison was that rare political bird – a politician who put principle ahead of politics. In 1992, he resigned as a minister after thirteen years in the Legislature when he disagreed with the government of the day.

5. **Bob Campbell:** Campbell hailed from the westernmost district on the island, and was known as "The Great West Wind." A religious man, Mr. Campbell always refused to accept the distribution of "discretionary" money on the Lord's Day just before an election. Upon his passing, he insisted that his money be divvied on Saturday. It was.

As a result of the Belfast melée, the Island government passed the Simultaneous Polling Act. An effort to discourage election-day mobs from congregating in a single location, the law decreed that elections in all jurisdictions be held on the same day.

Bio   GEORGE COLES: CAUTIOUS FATHER OF CONFEDERATION

Born to a modest farm family in 1810, George Coles made an indelible mark on Island politics. At age 19, a young George left his father's farm for England where he met and married Mercy Haine. Coles and his bride returned to the Island to raise their family of twelve. By 1836, Coles was a successful businessman working as a merchant, brewer and distiller, mill operator and farm manager.

In 1842, he was equally successful when he tried his hand at politics and was elected to the House of Assembly. Initially, Coles sided with the Tories and opposed the escheat movement. Over time, he came to agree with Reformers' demands for increased tenant rights and the sale of the land held by absentee landlords.

Reformer Coles spent much of the 1840s struggling for responsible government, an uphill battle that was resisted by colonial officials who feared that a popularly elected government would dismantle the absentee landholding system. In 1847, Island Governor Sir Henry Vere Huntley invited Coles to join the powerful and Tory-dominated Executive Council. Coles accepted but, disillusioned by his inability to influence the Council on the issue of land reform, resigned within the year, his commitment to responsible government very much intact.

In the 1850 election, the Reformers, led by Coles, won control of the Assembly and from this position continued the push for responsi-

NO THANK YOU CANADA

By 1864, the colonial government was desperate to solve the land issue. In September of that year, plans were made for a meeting in Charlottetown to discuss the prospect of Maritime union. The United Province of Canada, however, finagled its way into the meeting, changing the agenda to discussions of a broader North American Union. The PEI government was pleased; perhaps such a union would resolve the vexing land problem.

ble government. The efforts paid off. In 1851, PEI won responsible government and Coles was named Premier. As Premier, Coles cautiously continued to call for land reform. He publicly opposed Tenant League calls for outright escheat and his 1853 plan calling for the colony to purchase land from willing landlords failed.

Despite his failure to resolve the land issue by mid-century, Coles, regarded as a Liberal, remained Premier until his 1859 resignation. In the 1860s, he served as opposition leader and became a staunch supporter of a Confederation. But Coles' support was conditional. He insisted that a union agreement must include the federal purchase of lands held by absentee landholders. And so, when the Quebec Resolutions failed to provide for this, he adamantly opposed union. It was on this anti-Confederation platform that he was re-elected Liberal Premier in 1867 by those Islanders who opposed the 1867 terms of Confederation.

By this time, however, Coles' mental health was in decline and he again resigned as Premier. After spending time in a New Brunswick lunatic asylum, Coles died in Charlottetown in 1875. In death, George Coles became something of a folk hero, remembered for dedication to the interests of ordinary Islanders and his willingness to stand up to a bad Confederation deal.

PEI Premiers and Occupations

Premier	Party	Term	Occupation
Pre-Confederation			
George Coles	Liberal	1851-1854	Farmer/businessman
John Holl	Conservative	1854-1855	Landowner
George Coles	Liberal	1855-1859	Farmer/businessman
Edward Palmer	Conservative	1859-1863	Lawyer
John Hamilton Gray	Conservative	1863-1865	Army officer
James C. Pope	Conservative	1865-1867	Merchant/shipbuilder
George Coles	Liberal	1867-1869	Farmer/businessman
Joseph Hensley	Liberal	1869	Lawyer
Robert P. Haythorne	Liberal	1869-1870	Land owner
James C. Pope	Coalition	1870	Merchant/shipbuilder
Robert P. Haythorne	Liberal	1871-1873	Landowner
Post-Confederation			
James C. Pope	Conservative	1873	Merchant/shipbuilder
Lemuel C. Owen	Conservative	1873-1876	Merchant
Louis Henry Davies	Coalition	1876-1879	Lawyer
William W. Sullivan	Conservative	1879-1889	Lawyer
Neil McLeod	Conservative	1889-1891	Lawyer
Frederick Peters	Liberal	1891-1897	Lawyer
Alexander B. Warburton	Liberal	1897-1898	Lawyer
Donald Farquharson	Liberal	1899-1901	Teacher/businessman

Premier	Party	Term	Occupation
Post-Confederation (continued)			
Arthur Peters	Liberal	1901-1908	Lawyer
Francis L. Haszard	Liberal	1908-1911	Lawyer
H. James Palmer	Liberal	1911	Lawyer
John A. Mathieson	Conservative	1911-1917	Teacher/lawyer
Aubin E. Arsenault	Conservative	1917-1919	Teacher/lawyer
John Howatt Bell	Liberal	1919-1923	Lawyer
James D. Stewart	Conservative	1923-1927	Teacher/lawyer
Albert C. Saunders	Liberal	1927-1930	Lawyer
Walter M. Lea	Liberal	1930-1931	Farmer
James D. Stewart	Conservative	1931-1933	Teacher/lawyer
William J. P. MacMillan	Conservative	1933-1935	Physician
Walter M. Lea	Liberal	1935-1936	Farmer
Thane A. Campbell	Liberal	1936-1943	Lawyer
J. Walter Jones	Liberal	1943-1953	Teacher/farmer
Alex W. Matheson	Liberal	1953-1959	Lawyer
Walter R. Shaw	Progressive Conservative (PC)	1959-1966	Farmer
Alexander B. Campbell	Liberal	1966-1978	Lawyer
Bennett Campbell	Liberal	1978-1979	Teacher
Angus MacLean	PC	1979-1981	Farmer
James Lee	PC	1981-1986	Draftsman/real estate
Joe Ghiz	Liberal	1986-1993	Lawyer
Catherine Callbeck	Liberal	1993-1996	Businesswoman
Keith Milligan	Liberal	1996	Teacher/farmer
Pat Binns	PC	1996-2007	Businessman/farmer
Robert Ghiz	Liberal	2007-2015	Political lobbyist
Wade MacLauchlan	Liberal	2015-	Law Professor/President of UPEI

J. WALTER JONES
THE FARMER PREMIER

With an economy dominated by agriculture, it shouldn't be surprising that one of the most popular politicians in Island history was the "Farmer Premier." Born on April 14, 1878, J. Walter Jones was educated in agricultural studies at Acadia College and at the Ontario Agricultural College, from which he graduated in 1909. He then headed to Virginia, where he taught at Hampton Agricultural Institute and became Assistant Superintendent of the US Government Experimental Agricultural Farm in Arlington. Jones returned to PEI in 1913, eager to apply his agricultural training to the Island's rolling pastures. He experimented with cattle breeding, and was so successful that one of his Holsteins, the Abegweit Milady, set world records for milk and butterfat production. His contributions to cattle-breeding were recognized in May 1935 when Jones won the King's Silver Jubilee Medal for agriculture, giving him an international reputation in the cattle-breeding world.

Jones's agricultural career influenced his politics in a couple of ways. First, it delayed his entry into politics, as he did not contest a seat until after receiving his 1935 medal. Although successful in the 1935 election, Jones was relegated to the backbenches and it wasn't until he became Premier in 1943 that he formally became part of the Liberal establishment. The years of political isolation had conditioned Jones to be self-sufficient, and he tended to be more involved in aspects of government policy formation than had his predecessors, an attitude that served him well when he repealed the prohibition of alcohol against the wishes of the Island's teetotaling Lieutenant-Governor. Second, it allowed Jones to cast himself as the "Farmer Premier," which helped his political fortunes on agriculture-dependent PEI. Not only did this ingratiate him to the electorate, it gave Jones' voice greater authority when speaking on farming issues. He was, after all, a farmer, just like them.

The meetings at Charlottetown were decidedly low key. Indeed, the arrival of the Canadian delegates, including bigwigs John A. Macdonald, George Brown, Georges Cartier and Alexander Galt, was hardly noticed by Islanders who were far more interested in a circus visiting Charlottetown that day.

Nevertheless, the Canadians made a strong case for Confederation, indicating that the new federal government might ante up to purchase the lands of absentee overseers. A second round of Confederation talks followed in October 1864 and the Confederation deal was inked.

In the end, though, PEI was not interested. The proposal did not include the discussed federal concession to buy Island property. Given their relatively small numbers, Islanders opposed the "rep by pop" principle at the heart of the proposed new federal system that would allot the Island just five seats in the legislature.

Islanders also feared increased taxes and asserted that those levies would not benefit the Island, but rather pay for the mainland railroad. When New Brunswick, Nova Scotia, Quebec and Ontario entered Confederation on July 1, 1867, PEI retained its independence.

CONVINCED OF CONFEDERATION

In the years following 1867, Islanders continued to be wary of Confederation. When Ottawa sweetened the pot with better terms in 1869, Islanders rejected these overtures as well. Nevertheless, links between the independent Island and the newly-minted Canada grew. The Island was soon placed under the jurisdiction of the Canadian Governor General and, in 1871, PEI adopted Canada's system of coinage.

In the meantime, as the British urged the Island to join the union, faltering Island economic fortunes gave Confederation a boost. Not long

Did you know...

. . . that Aubin-Edmond Arsenault was not just PEI's first Acadian premier? He was also the first Acadian premier in Canada.

after 1867, high hopes of renewed free trade with the United States were dashed. As well, in the years since 1867, "railway fever" had swept PEI and a web of railroads criss-crossed the Island, leaving the small colony wallowing in debt. Suddenly a federal plan that promised to assume railroad debt became enticing and a number of Island politicians changed their tunes.

Premier Robert Haythorne made the first step, journeying to Ottawa in 1873, where he secured a new Confederation offer. Later that year, with Haythorne's successor James Pope at the helm, PEI agreed to a Confederation agreement with terms that were only slightly better than those rejected in 1867.

Ottawa assumed PEI's massive railway debt, increased its debt allowance, granted a subsidy to compensate for its lack of Crown lands, agreed to establish a year round communication (a ferry) with the mainland and increased to six its share of seats in the House of Commons. Most importantly to many, however, the 1873 Confederation deal promised to solve once and for all the long-outstanding land issue, as it provided the Island a loan of $800,000 to purchase the estates of the absentee landowners.

POLITICAL GEOGRAPHY
- Number of counties: 3 (Kings, Prince and Queens)
- Number of cities: 2 (Charlottetown and Summerside)
- Number of towns: 7 (Alberton, Cornwall, Georgetown, Kensington, Montague, Souris and Stratford)

Did you know...

... that on a visit to PEI in August 2000, Prime Minister Jean Chrétien was greeted with a PIE to the face? The pastry-pitching protester was sentenced to 30 days in jail, but had his sentence reduced to eight days, already served.

- Municipalities: 66
- Indian reserves: 4 (Morell, Scotchfort, Rocky Point and Lennox Island)
- Provincial electoral districts: 27
- Federal voting districts: 4
- Location of provincial legislature: Charlottetown

Source: Government of PEI; Elections PEI.

Bio CATHERINE CALLBECK

Catherine Callbeck was born in Bedeque in 1939. As a young woman she put her Bachelor of Commerce and Education degrees to work, teaching business in Canada and the United States. In 1968, she returned to her Island hometown and took the helm of her family's business, Callbeck's of Central Bedeque.

In 1974, Callbeck successfully ran for the provincial Liberal party and was promptly named to Cabinet, becoming Minister of Health and Social Services and Minister Responsible for Disabled Persons. Four years later, she resigned from provincial politics, returning to her family's business.

Her political hiatus lasted a decade. In 1988, she returned to politics, this time on the federal stage. Elected MP for Malpeque, she had an active role in the Liberal opposition in Ottawa. Four years later she changed her political course, returning yet again to PEI politics by winning the leadership of the provincial Liberal party.

In the 1993 provincial election – an historic contest that for the first time in Canadian history featured three provincial parties all headed by women – she won the Premier's seat and became the first woman in Canadian history to be elected as Premier of a province. In 1996, her support waning, Callbeck retired from politics and returned to her family business. Within a year, however, she was back in Ottawa, appointed by Prime Minister Chrétien to the Senate. Senator Callbeck continues to serve her constituents from the Upper House.

PARTIES

Prince Edward Island is home to three political parties: the Progressive Conservatives, the Liberals and the New Democratic Party. Only the Liberals and the Conservatives have ever formed a government.

- Number of Liberal governments: 18
- Number of Conservative governments: 13
- Number of coalition governments: 1

CURRENT ADMINISTRATION

- Premier: Wade MacLauchlan,the province's 31st premier
- Party: Liberal
- Date sworn in: February 23, 2015
- Number of MLAs: 27
- Liberals: 18
- Progressive Conservatives: 8
- Green Party; 1
- Female MLAs: 5
- Voter turnout in 2015: 85.9 percent
- Lt. Governor: Hon. H. Frank Lewis

Source: Legislative Assembly of PEI; Elections PEI.

Did you know...

... that despite the power outages and travel mayhem caused by Hurricane Juan on September 30, 2003, the provincial election held that day recorded an 83 percent voter turn out?

PREMIER PRIMER

- Number of Premiers who have served since 1873: 32
- First Liberal Premier: George Coles
- First Conservative Premier: Edward Palmer
- First farmer Premier: George Coles
- Youngest Premier: Alex Campbell, aged 32
- Longest serving Premier: Alex Campbell, 12 years, 4 months
- Number of female Premiers: 1 (Catherine Callbeck)
- First Acadian Premier: Aubin-Edmond Arsenault

Source: CanadaHistory.com.

FRANCHISE FACTS

- Year responsible government was implemented: 1851
- Year women got the right to vote: 1921
- Year Natives on reserve lost the right to vote: 1922
- Year in which this right was returned: 1963
- Voting age: 18
- Residency: One must "ordinarily" be a resident of PEI for at least six months before election is called.

Source: Government of Canada, Depository Services Program.

ELECTION DAY

Municipal elections are held every four years, on the first Monday in November. The next municipal elections are scheduled for Monday, November 5, 2018.

Did you know...

... that Prince Edward Island is the first province in Canada to elect a premier of non-European descent? Joseph Atallah Ghiz, whose family is of Syro-Lebanese descent, was elected Premier in 1986 and served until 1993.

FEDERAL POLITICS
- Number of Islanders who have been Prime Minister: 0
- Number of MPs in Ottawa: 4
- Number who are female: 1
- Number of Senators to which PEI is entitled: 4
- Current number of Island Senators: 3
- Number who are female: 1

PARLIAMENT HILL INSTITUTION
He has spent more than a quarter century on Parliament Hill and it's been said that you will learn something new every time he opens his mouth. Mike Duffy was born in Charlottetown in 1946 and has since become synonymous with news on CTV, having appeared on each of that corporation's news broadcasts.

Among his many accolades are the ACTRA award, a spot in the Canadian Association of the Broadcasters Hall of Fame, honorary degrees from UPEI and New York's Niagara University, and two nominations by the *Washington Journalism Review* for its Best in Business award. The *Toronto Star* has described this PEI native as "the reporter to whom other journalists listen for insight."

In 2014, Prince Edward Island senator, Mike Duffy, was charged with 31 criminal offenses, including fraud, breach of trust and bribery. He had quit the Conservative caucus in 2013 amid this scandal. After sitting as an independent for a short while, he was suspended without pay for two years.

Did you know...
. . . that Prime Minister William Lyon McKenzie King was first elected to the House of Commons in a 1919 by-election in which he offered himself as the candidate for Prince, PEI? He was uncontested and his seat acclaimed.

WOMEN IN PEI POLITICS

Island women got the right to vote federally in 1918, and to vote provincially in 1921. It would, however, be another 30 years before an Island woman would run as a provincial candidate.

- 1951: Hilda Ramsay (CCF) is the first woman to vie for election to the Legislative Assembly.
- 1955: Florence Elsie Inman is the first Island woman appointed to the Senate.
- 1960: Mary Bernard is the first woman elected chief of the Lennox Island First Nation.
- 1961: Mary Margaret Smith MacDonald (PC) is the first Island woman elected to the House of Commons.
- 1968: Dorothy Corrigan is the first woman elected mayor of Charlottetown.
- 1970: Jean Canfield (Liberal) is the first Island woman elected to the Legislative Assembly. Two years later she becomes the first female Cabinet Minister (PEI Housing Authority).
- 1972: The PEI Advisory Council on the Status of Women is established.
- 1979: Frances Perry is the first woman elected mayor of Summerside.
- 1983: Marion Reid (PC) becomes the first woman to serve as speaker of the Provincial Legislature.
- 1990: Pat Mella (PC) is the first woman to lead a political party on PEI.
- 1990: Marion Reid is the first woman appointed Lieutenant Governor for Prince Edward Island.
- 1993: Catherine Callbeck is named Liberal leader and becomes the first female Premier of PEI. Later that year she wins an election to

Did you know...

. . . that PEI has a total of 566 elected officials for a population of 138,307?

become the Island's — and the nation's — first female premier-elect.

- 1993: Pat Mella (PC) is the first woman on PEI to hold the position of Leader of the Official Opposition.
- 2004: Lennox Island First Nation elects an all-female Band Council with Darlene Bernard as Chief.
- 2004: Mildred Dover (PC) becomes the first woman to be appointed Attorney General.

Despite being at an all-time high, Island women, who make up 51 percent of the population, remain underrepresented in government. As of 2015, women occupy approximately 20 percent of provincial legislature seats and account for fewer than 25 percent of elected municipal councillors. PEI has one female Member of Parliament.

Source: PEI Coalition for Women in Government; Elections PEI; Government of PEI, Advisory Council on the Status of Women.

THE POLITICAL LEFT

Third parties have never had much success in Prince Edward Island. In the 1940s, however, Islanders voted for candidates of the Co-operative Commonwealth Federation (CCF) party. Founded in western Canada after the Great Depression, its leftist platform was a socialist one, based on the tenets of socialized banks and public ownership of transportation, communication and resources.

In the 1940s, this platform appealed to Islanders who themselves had recently suffered hard years of recession. In the election of 1943, five CCF candidates ran in the province and in 1947, a record 17 CCFers offered themselves for election. None succeeded.

In 1951, the Island CCF made history when CCFer Hilda Ramsay offered herself as a candidate in the provincial election, becoming the first woman in Island history to run for public office. It was not to be. The past repeated itself and Ramsay and other CCF candidates lost their races.

When the CCF was transformed into the New Democratic Party (NDP), it remained on the Island's political radar, albeit as a small blip. It was not until 1996 that NDPer Dr. Herb Dickieson made history when his electoral win made him the one and only third party candidate in Island history to win a seat in the provincial legislature.

Weblinks

To find out more about Island politics, check out these web pages maintained by the three major political parties.

Progressive Conservative Party of PEI
www.pcparty.pe.ca

Liberal Party of PEI
http://pei.liberal.ca/

New Democratic Party of PEI
http://www.ndppei.ca/

Then and Now

We all belong to a place and a time in history. What is remarkable is just how radically things change. From the pre-industrial age through to the modern age, one only need reflect back a generation to just those changes. From the introduction of cell phones to party lines to one-room school houses to the Société Educative de l'Ile-du-Prince-Edouard, this chapter is walk back through time that tells where we've come from.

POPULATION THEN AND NOW
(PERCENTAGE OF CANADIAN POPULATION)

- 1748 700 (.37 percent)
- 1851 62,678 (2.57 percent)
- 1901 103,259 (1.92 percent)
- 1951 98,429 (.7 percent)
- 2008 139,818 (.4 percent)
- 2014: 145,237 (.5 percent)

LIFE EXPECTANCY

Over the past century, the life expectancy of Islanders has been on the rise. One thing that hasn't changed, however, is that Island women outlive men.

	Men	Women
1921	59.2	61.1
1951	69.7	72.7
1991	72.5	80.7
2005	77.4	82.1
2013:	78.0	83.0

Source: Statistics Canada.

POPULATION DENSITY (CANADA)

1871	16.62 people/km^2 (1.06)
1901	18.25 people/km^2 (1.55)
1951	17.40 people/km^2 (3.88)
2006	23.9 people/km^2 (3.5)
2014:	24.7 people/km^2 (3.87)

Source: Statistics Canada, Historical Statistics of Canada.

PEI FARMS, THEN AND NOW

Farm Acreage

1881	1,127,000
1901	1,195,000
1951	1,095,000
2006	619,885
2013	594,000

Average Farm Size

1901	87 acres
2006	365 acres
2014	Few to 3000 acres

Did you know...

... that before intensive agriculture changed the face of the land, PEI was covered by a dense blanket of broadleaf, deciduous trees, especially American beech, sugar maple, yellow birch and red oak, mixed with fir, spruce, tamarack, some white pine, hemlock and white cedar?

Number of Farms

1881	13,629
1901	13,748
1951	10,137
2006	1,700
2014	1,500

Sources: Statistics Canada; Government of PEI.

VEHICLE REGISTRATIONS

1913	26
1921	1,750
1931	7,744
1951	16,896
2007	97,032
2013	111,425

Source: Statistics Canada.

UNIVERSITY, THEN AND NOW
(FULLTIME UNDERGRADUATE ENROLMENT)

1920	107
1950	270
1960	563
1970	1,755
2006	3,783
2013	4,300

Source: Statistics Canada, Historical Statistics of Canada.

Did you know...

. . . that PEI has extremely strict land ownership rules, a throw-back to the land issues that have plagued the Island throughout its history? Residents and corporations are limited to maximum holdings of 400 and 1200 hectares, respectively. Non-resident property owners also pay higher property taxes.

RURAL VS. URBAN

A testament to its agrarian past and present, every resident of the Island lived rurally in 1851. By 1901, this was down to a still-considerable 86 percent and by 2001, the population balance between urban and rural was still skewed in favour of the countryside. In that year, 55 percent of Islanders lived rurally.

Source: Statistics Canada.

PRIMARY AND SECONDARY SCHOOL ENROLMENT, THEN AND NOW

1867	13,000
1900	21,000
1950	19,000
1970	31,000
2003	23,132
2014	20,164

Source: Statistics Canada; Canadian Council on Social Development; Government of Prince Edward Island.

DIFFICULT CROSSING

A phenomenon unique to the Northumberland Strait is the presence of what Islanders call the 'lolly.' Lolly is a term given to a large amount of floating snow or ground-up ice in the middle of the Strait.

In the 19th century, iceboats were used to traverse the frozen Strait, carrying mail and other necessities to an ice-locked Island. These small, lightweight vessels were equipped with oars, runners and straps. In open water they could be rowed, but when impeded by ice, they could be hauled across frozen sections of the Strait.

When ice conditions were good, this journey could be relatively easy. However, the presence of unstable lollies proved a huge nuisance. If a boat came across such a lolly it could neither be rowed, nor could its occupants get out of the boat to pull it across the slushy section.

LEGACY OF SLAVERY

Although it is a little known fact, slavery was once practiced on PEI. In the 1780s, a small group of Loyalist settlers brought with them their African-American slaves, men and women who were 'owned' and whose enslavement continued on the Island's red soil. By the early 1800s, slave-holding was rare on the Island but not officially abolished until 1825. The legacy of slavery cast a long shadow, with racism and discrimination being the bane of Black Islanders long after slavery was banned.

Take 5 GEORGES ARSENAULT'S TOP 5
INFLUENTIAL ACADIANS ON PEI

Georges Arsenault has published extensively on the history and traditions of the Acadians of his native province. He is the author of *The Acadians of Prince Edward Island: 1720-1980* and has contributed several articles to *The Island Magazine* and the *Dictionary of Canadian Biography*. For 15 years, he was the host of Radio-Canada's morning program in Prince Edward Island.

1. **Gilbert Buote**. An educator, he became the Island's first Acadian newspaper editor and historian.

2. **Rev. Pierre-Paul Arsenault**. An outstanding leader, he promoted education, cooperation and heritage preservation.

3. **Aubin Edmond Arsenault**. Politician and judge, Arsenault was the first Acadian to become premier of a Canadian province.

4. **Prof. J. Henri Blanchard**. An educator and historian who for many years was the pillar of the Société Saint-Thomas-d'Aquin, the Island's chief institutional voice.

5. **Angèle Arsenault**. A singer and songwriter of international acclaim.

In the 19th century, a number of Black Islanders settled in the "Bog" district of Charlottetown, a community in the city's west end that was founded by former slave Samuel Martin. Life in the Bog was difficult. Residents — known as "Boggies" — lived in impoverished huts, their plight ignored by city officials. Boggies were rich in community spirit as witnessed by the existence of their own school, church and hockey team. By the 20th century, though, the Bog population fell. Lured to New England and elsewhere, Boggies left their Island community for larger urban centres.

Source: Black Islanders: Prince Edward Island's Historical Black Community.

WILLIAM ELLIS

Born in 1774 in England, William Ellis was a pioneer of the ship building industry on PEI, which was vitally important to the Island's development in the 19th century. Ellis arrived on PEI in 1818, landholder in Lot 12, Prince County. Although records of the day are neither complete nor precise, it is clear that he was responsible for building many dozens of sailing ships, leading the industry on the Island between 1818 and his death in 1855.

EDUCATION, THEN AND NOW

During its early history, Island children were sent abroad to be educated. By the 19th century, Islanders were calling for local schools to be established so their children could be educated at home. In 1804, Kent College was established at the site of modern day Holland College, and 16 years later, the Island's first public school opened

Did you know...

. . . that 19th century passengers who had to leave the Island in winter in an iceboat paid one of two fares? Those who pitched in and helped pull the vessel over the ice paid $2, while the lazier passengers who stayed in the boat the whole trip had to pay $4.

in Charlottetown. This was followed by a flurry of education acts passed to establish a public school system. In 1831, a new college, St. Andrew's — later renamed St. Dunstan's University — opened its doors in Charlottetown, and the Central Academy, later the Prince of Wales College, began offering classes in 1836. Reformer Premier George Coles, convinced of the desirability of responsible government and of the need of an educated electorate, blazed educational trails with his 1852 Education Act, making PEI the first jurisdiction in the British empire to offer free, state-supported public schooling.

Irish Moss

As the production of mussel mud plummeted in the 1940s, another harvest emerged to take its place. With World War II there came an international need for chondrus crispus or, as many Islanders know it, Irish Moss. What is so special about this seaweed? Irish Moss contains carrageenan, a substance that is central to the manufacture of such food and household staples as toothpaste, shampoo, beer and dairy products, in which it acts as a gelling and stabilizing element.

At the height of the industry's popularity in the 1970s, PEI was providing more than a third of the world's carrageenan. Whole communities of Islanders harvested the plant. After stormy weather had churned up the grass, Islanders, aided by horse teams, dragged baskets along the seabed and scooped up the greenery.

Since its peak, the Irish Moss industry has been on the decline, the result of over-harvesting and the discovery of alternative sources of carrageenan. Nevertheless, the grass may still be fairly green for the Island's Irish Moss industry. Research suggests that Irish Moss contains properties that may help in the fight against HIV, the virus that causes AIDS.

In the 20th century, Islanders demanded school reform, and in particular called for schools that offered agricultural training. And so, in 1920, as the Island recovered from the Great War, the PEI Agricultural and Technical School was established. In the 1960s, vocational and technical training schools opened across the province.

1969 was a big year for Island education. Holland College opened and the University of Prince Edward Island was founded with the merger of Prince of Wales College and St. Dunstan's University.

In 1972, the public school system was transformed. Five regional boards replaced numerous school districts, and the 189 schools operating in 1971 were consolidated and reduced to 70 by 1994. In 1986, the Atlantic Veterinary College opened its doors and, as of 1992, Francophone Islanders have been able to get a French post-secondary education at the Société Educative de l'Ile-du-Prince-Edouard. In 1994, the five regional school boards were reduced to three, one French and two English.

Acadians

The Acadians have had a long and, at times, difficult history on Prince Edward Island. In 1720, France first colonized the Island, then known as Ile St. Jean, with 300 settlers. This colony waned, but a small number of Acadians remained, centred at Port LaJoie. By 1728, the Island was home to 297 French residents and efforts were made to entice French settlers from the Acadia mainland. A few accepted the invitation, and by 1748, 735 Acadians lived on Ile St. Jean.

When war between France and England erupted in 1744, tensions escalated between mainland Acadians and the British, then in control of Nova Scotia. Acadians were instructed to swear an unconditional oath to the British and when they refused, there were rumours of deportation. Fearing this repercussion, many Acadians moved to Ile St. Jean, tripling the population of the small French colony. When the Great Expulsion began in Nova Scotia in August 1755, even more Acadians sought refuge on the Island and by the following year, almost 4,400 Acadians called the Island home.

It did not remain a haven for long, however. In 1758, British officials deported the Island's Acadian residents, uprooting some 3,000 settlers. The lucky ones made it to France; a doomed 700 died in shipwrecks.

After the Deportation, the British assumed control of the now anglicized St. John's Island, changing the name of Port LaJoie to Fort Amherst. When the war ended in 1763, Acadians were permitted to return to St. John's Island. Thanks to the 1767 land lottery, however, Acadians were relegated, like all Island farmers, to tenant status. While they eked out farming livings under these conditions, they also became adept fishermen. The Acadians lived busy but quiet lives, prohibited by law from engaging in politics until 1830.

In the late 19th century, Island Acadians joined their cultural counterparts elsewhere in an "Acadian Renaissance" – a time of renewed political and cultural strength for the proud and determined Island Acadians.

FOX FARMING

From the late 19th century until the 1940s, fox farming was one of the Island's most lucrative industries. The furry critter at the heart of the industry was the silver-black fox, a mutant breed of the wild red fox. Their luxurious pelts were highly valued by the fashion-conscious, with pelts fetching between $350 and $1,000.

Charles Dalton and Robert Oulton opened the first fox farm on the Island in 1890 and were wildly successful, so much so, in fact, that Dalton would be able to parlay his successes into political clout, becoming Lieutenant-Governor of PEI four decades later. In order to achieve the rare feat of successfully breeding fur-bearing wild animals in captivity, Island fox ranchers developed innovative designs to mimic the natural habitat of the fox. The Islanders' techniques paved the way for international ranchers and were adopted over the world.

At the height of the boom, pelts were worth as much as $2,000 each, with a single pair of foxes selling for $35,000 between 1910 and 1914. By the start of World War I, 85 percent of the world's captive silver foxes lived on PEI. By 1923, 448 fox farms peppered the Island, making it the largest fox fur producer in the world. That year PEI raked in $2,689,772 from fox farming.

A victim of the fickle fads of fashion, increased animal rights activism and an over-saturated pelt market, the industry was in decline by the end of World War II. Island fox farmers were devastated and never recovered. By 2004, there were just ten fox farms left on the Island.

Source: Statistics Canada; Legion Magazine; Economic Geography.

Did you know...

... that between 1800 and 1880 Island ship builders built almost 4,000 ships, making shipbuilding the driving force of the Island economy for almost a century?

ISLAND CONNECTIONS

Canada's two island provinces — Prince Edward Island and Newfoundland — have had a longstanding trade relationship. During the 18th and early 19th centuries, Newfoundland buyers gave breath to the nascent Prince Edward Island lumber and shipbuilding trades. Moreover, Newfoundland relied heavily on imported foodstuffs, most of which came from PEI. A March 15, 1819 edition of the Prince Edward Island *Gazette* made this abundantly clear: "Newfoundland is entirely supplied by this Island with live cattle, fowls, corn, potatoes, and even garden stuff."

This exchange of goods between the two islands continued into the 20th century. From 1905 to 1918, Ottawa subsidized a route from Charlottetown to Placentia, with stops at a variety of Nova Scotia ports along the way. Despite the withdrawal of federal support following World War I, trade between the two islands continued, and by the 1920s, ships laden with foodstuffs destined for Newfoundland were a common sight at such Prince Edward Island ports as Montague and Murray Harbour.

The outbreak of World War II altered the trade relationship. Ships once dedicated to the Newfoundland route were now commandeered for the war effort, and Sydney, Nova Scotia, became the focal point for trade. At the same time, the presence of Canadian and American servicemen in Newfoundland meant that demand for imported foodstuffs — foodstuffs PEI could supply — had never been higher.

Over the course of the war, PEI Premier Walter Jones lobbied the federal government on behalf of Island agriculture. Jones' efforts paid off. For a while, Ottawa mandated that only beef cattle from PEI could be exported to Newfoundland. In addition, Jones was able in 1946 to secure from Ottawa a new modern freighter for the Charlottetown-St. John's route — the aptly named *Island Connector*.

Did you know...

... that until 1924, Island drivers drove on the left side of the road?

They Said It

PARTY LINES

In 1885, just a decade after Mr. Bell invented the telephone, PEI's first phone was tested in Charlottetown. A year later, Summerside got its first phone line.

In 1920, regular commercial phone services became available when the Bell Telephone Company began to service the Island, and two years later the Telephone Company of Prince Edward Island was born. In 1929, the Island Telephone Company Ltd. was incorporated. In 1948, PEI made phone history when the first commercial microwave link in the world connected the Island and Nova Scotia. By 1977, all Islanders had dial phones.

The party line would, however, remain a lasting feature of Island phone service. Many a rural Islander recalls the party lines that allowed them, if so inclined, to listen in on their neighbours' phone conversations. Potentially a form of sneaky recreation, the party line connected Islanders who often lived remote from their neighbours. Over time, the number of party lines diminished until the last one was eliminated in the late 1990s.

Did you know...

. . . that "mussel mud" is more accurately "oyster mud"?
Contrary to popular belief, the main ingredient of this nutrient-rich fertilizer is not the shell of mussels but rather oyster shells.

CAR CONTROVERSY

Islanders, more than any other Canadians, resisted the coming of automobiles. The arrival of cars on the Island – there were five "horseless carriages" traveling PEI roads in 1905 – caused a hailstorm of opposition. So opposed were horse-loving Islanders to cars, that a 1908 law banned them altogether.

W.K. Rogers challenged the ban, defiantly continuing to drive his car, though in the end he failed to force a change of law. In 1913, when invited to weigh in on the subject in a plebiscite, Islanders voted in favour of ending the ban, though there was a sharp rural-urban divide. Rural people voted for a continuation of the ban; Island urbanites for its lifting.

In the aftermath of the plebiscite, it was decided that if 75 percent of local voters agreed, roads in a given region could be opened to cars. In 1919, the last road closed to vehicular traffic – the road from Tracadie to Mount Stewart – was opened, once and for all bringing an end to the ban on cars.

THE FIX IS IN

The 1997 completion of the Confederation Bridge linking PEI and New Brunswick marked the realization of a decades-old dream to have a fixed link between the Island and the Canadian mainland. Talk of a fixed link first surfaced in the 19th century and resurfaced on numerous occasions before becoming reality:

- 1870s: George Howlan lobbies for the construction of a railway tunnel beneath the ocean.
- 1905: Tunnel advocate Alfred Burke travels to Ottawa to lobby for a tunnel. The federal government promises to consider the idea, but takes no action.

They Said It

- 1960s: Reflecting the success of Nova Scotia's recently completed Canso Causeway, supporters advocate the building of a similar rock-fill causeway between New Brunswick and the Island. Approach roads and railway lines are constructed in anticipation, but the project is abandoned in 1969 in favour of improved ferry service.
- 1982: Public Works Canada (PWC) reviews a proposed bridge design with an estimated cost of $640 million.
- 1985-86: PWC receives three unsolicited proposals from the private sector. Bids included proposals for a bridge, a tunnel and a causeway.
- 1987: PWC solicits proposals for a fixed link.
- 1988: In a January plebiscite, Islanders vote in favour of a fixed link by a margin of 59.4 percent to 40.6 percent.
- 1992: Strait Crossing is selected for the project.
- 1994-97: 5,000 construction workers work year round. The bridge has a final price tag of $1 billion.
- 1996: The name Confederation Bridge is chosen in the aftermath of the narrow Quebec sovereignty referendum of the previous year.
- 1997: On May 31, the Confederation Bridge officially opens.

Did you know...

. . . that the ferry *The Abegweit*, that carried cars and passengers between Borden, PEI, and Cape Tourmentine, New Brunswick from 1947 until 1982 now serves as the clubhouse for the Columbia Yacht Club in Chicago?

They Said It

> " *I think a majority of Islanders have expressed a desire to have a fixed link connecting PEI and the mainland. It is a clear mandate to negotiate with the federal government while respecting the concerns of the many Islanders who voted against it.*"
>
> **– PEI Premier Joe Ghiz in his official statement following the fixed link plebiscite in 1992.**

A BASKET CASE

Basket socials were once a common social activity on PEI. On an appointed evening of revelry, girls and women in a community would fill ornately decorated baskets with homemade goodies or bake a pie. The baskets and pies would then be offered up to the highest bidding male, the proceeds going to local community projects.

Boyfriends would strive to buy their sweethearts' baskets and the two lovebirds could share its contents. If an unattached man were sweet on a girl he would bid on her basket to create a dating opportunity. If the crowd perceived his interest, they would force up the price of the basket in a bidding contest, making the amorous young man pay a considerable amount for his date.

Did you know...

> . . . that the late Island Premier Joseph Ghiz, who very publicly guarded his feelings on the bridge issue, is said to have voted "No" to the fixed link in the 1988 plebiscite on the issue?

MUSSEL MUD

PEI's economy has long rested on agriculture — particularly the growth of its world famous potatoes. By the mid-19th century, a definitively Island farming technique — made possible by an Island invention — revolutionized and defined farming practices on PEI. This was the use of mussel mud, a potent fertilizing mud found on the edges of tidal rivers.

Laced with crushed shells, mussel mud contains lime that was lacking in Island soil. Innovative Islanders developed a horse-operated machine to harvest this mud. By the 1860s, farmers were harvesting mussel mud in winter by digging it off the top of riverbank ice. For almost a century, this homegrown agricultural innovation was widely credited with boosting Island potato yields. In the 1940s, however, the production and use of mussel mud plummeted, undermined by the growing availability of inexpensive lime and potato buyers' assertions that mussel mud caused scabs on the lucrative tubers.

Weblinks

PEI Museums
www.islandregister.com/museums.html
Want to see PEI's history in person? Check out one of the Island's many museums, listed here.

Archives and Records Office of Prince Edward Island
http://www.edu.pe.ca/paro/
Want to do some genealogical research or just learn more about PEI's history online? Start here, at the wesbite of the provincial Archives and Records Office.

Community Museums Association of Prince Edward Island
http://www.virtualmuseum.ca/Exhibitions/
PrinceEdwardIslandHarvest/fox_e/foxpast01.html
Learn more about the historic harvests that have been the backbone of PEI's economy through the years.

The First People

ORIGINS

The first people of PEI are the Mi'kmaq. Their ancestors, the so-called "Paleo-Indians," settled the region at least 10,000 years ago, a time when the Island was part of the mainland. About 5,000 years ago sea levels rose, cutting the Island off from the mainland and making the ancestors of the Mi'kmaq the first Islanders.

MI'KMA'KI

The Mi'kmaq know PEI as Epekwitk, which literally means "lying down flat," but is often translated to mean "cradled in the waves." Epekwitk is one region of a seven-part Mi'kmaq homeland called Mi'kma'ki, which includes all of Atlantic Canada. This homeland is governed by a three part political system consisting of local (community) chiefs, district chiefs (one for each of the seven districts) and a Grand Chief — based in Cape Breton — who is responsible for the spiritual and political well being of all of Mi'kma'ki.

Source: Native Council of Prince Edward Island.

CARTIER CALLING

News of the Europeans landing at present-day Newfoundland and Labrador in the late 15th century probably traveled through Mi'kmaq

They Said It

lines of communication, as coastal Mi'kmaq traded on a small scale with European fisherman. In 1534, Jacques Cartier was the first European to record an encounter with the Mi'kmaq of Epekwitk.

That June, as his ship sailed near the Island's coastline, he and his crewmates spied boatloads of Mi'kmaq. Clearly accustomed to bartering with Europeans, the Mi'kmaq motioned to Cartier their desire to trade. Although weather conditions prevented a meeting on that first day, on following and subsequent days Cartier and his crew traded knives and iron for Mi'kmaq furs.

SPIRITUAL TRADITIONS

Like many Aboriginals, the Mi'kmaq are animistic and believe humans to be part of a multi-layered universe in which all animals and objects have a spiritual essence. The physical and spiritual worlds interact continuously. This philosophy forms the belief among the Mi'kmaq that all parts of a killed animal must be preserved and respected. Failure to respect the animal might result in hunting scarcity.

People are not isolated from the spirit world; some can communicate with it. The Mi'kmaq call such a person a puion. Aided by a medicine bag containing sacred items such as bones, pebbles and carvings, these spirit guides communicate with the spirit world to learn the locations of game and fish, as well as predict the weather.

LANDLESS

When the colony of PEI was divided by lottery into 67 lots, the Mi'kmaq received no legal title to any of their homeland. It was only thanks to a clerical error that inadvertently omitted Lennox Island from the survey, and to the goodwill of a landholder, that the 1,320-acre Lennox Island eventually became the unofficial home to PEI's landless Mi'kmaq in 1772.

Mi'kmaq Place Names

Official name	Mi'kmaq name
Bedeque	Eptek (a hot place)
Charlottetown Harbour	Booksak (narrow passage between cliffs)
China Point	Abadomkeak (sandy shore winding and turning)
East Point	Kespemenagek (the end of the island)
Fullertons	Apsogonigatetjg (small legs)
Hillsborough River	Elsetgog (flowing close by high rocks)
Indian River	Lipangotitjg (portage over a sand bar)
Malpeque	Makpaak (large bay)
Miminegash	Elmenigetjg (forward land)
Misgouche	Menisgotig (little marshy place)
New London Bay	Kicheboogwek Booktaba (bay of shoals, enclosed bay)
Panmure Island	Goesogongiag (sand bar)
Rice Point	Segunakadech (little ground nut place)
St. Peter's Bay	Pogoosumkek Booktaba (bay of clams)
St. Peter's Island	Baslooakade (haunt of the seacow)
Savage Harbour	Kadotpichk (eel water place or eel screen)
Souris	Sgoltjoegatig (frog resort)
West Point	Mooeak (sea duck)
Wood Islands	Menesg (grassy)

A century later, in 1870, Lennox Island was purchased by the England-based Anti Slavery and Aborigines Protection Society and the land was held in trust for the Mi'kmaq until it was made a reserve in 1912.

WABANAKI CONFEDERACY

The Wabanaki Confederacy is a political alliance consisting of the Natives of northeastern North America. Meaning "dawnland people," the Wabanaki alliance included the Penobscot (of present day Maine), Passamaqoddy, Maliseet and Mi'kmaq.

The Confederacy was established in the 17th century, in response to the political and military threat posed by enemy Iroquois. The Confederacy met to preserve peace, develop concerted political and military strategies and negotiate with other Natives and Europeans. It also served as a cultural connector between these First Nations. In 1862, the Wabanaki Confederacy officially disbanded, although informal alliances between these nations continue the Wabanaki relationship.

POLITICS

The political leaders of the First People of PEI, Saqamaws, were men chosen by a community to offer political advice. Although a Saqamaw's position might be handed down from father to son, or uncle to nephew, merit was more important and a leader had to prove his worth. One way he could do this was by sharing the spoils of his hunting with his whole community, ensuring their collective well being. A Saqamaw did not rule dictatorially or autocratically. Rather, political decisions were made using persuasion and consensus.

THE MI'KMAQ STAR

The eight-pointed star is an ancient Mi'kmaq symbol of unity. It represents the sun, a powerful figure in Mi'kmaq spirituality. In addition, the eight points are said to represent the seven Mi'kmaq districts and the 1752 treaty that connected the Mi'kmaq and the British crown.

LANGUAGE

The Mi'kmaq language, known by speakers as Mi'kmawi'simk, is a dialect of the Algonquian language stock, one of the two main Northeastern Aboriginal languages (the other is Iroquoian). Today

Take 5 LENNOX ISLAND FIRST NATION CHIEF DARLENE BERNARD'S
TOP FIVE MI'KMAQ RIGHTS ISSUES

Chief Darlene Bernard was first elected Chief of the Lennox Island First Nation in April 2001. In February 2007, her mandate was renewed and she is now serving her third term as Chief. Under her respected leadership, Lennox Island has emerged as a progressive First Nation.

Chief Bernard has worked diligently to address outstanding Mi'kmaq rights issues across PEI. Chief Bernard lives on Lennox Island with her husband, Don, and three youngest children. Her eldest daughter resides in Summerside with her husband and her first grandchild.

1. **Aboriginal Title:** The Canadian government has failed to recognize Mi'kmaq Aboriginal Title to the land. The Mi'kmaq of PEI believe recognition is long overdue.

2. **Citizenship:** Ottawa has defined what it is to have status. Bernard says it is time for the Mi'kmaq of PEI to define their own criterion of band membership.

3. **Management of resources:** The Mi'kmaq believe they have inalienable rights to Island resources, and should establish management strategies for them.

4. **Government to government issues:** Mi'kmaq are very adamant with having voices heard in tripartite talks with the federal and provincial governments. She says the right of Mi'kmaq self-determination should be recognized by all parties.

5. **Self-determination and self-government:** Bernard says the Mi'kmaq of PEI believe that they have the right to determine their own futures and government structures.

They Said It

the Mi'kmaq language has a written alphabet, but it was formerly conveyed orally or through pictographs. Contrary to popular misconception, Mi'kmaq pictographs are not derived from Ancient Egyptian or Mayan hieroglyphs – they are North American in origin.

BIRCH BARK CANOE

This ingenious vessel allowed the Island Mi'kmaq to travel the tempestuous coastlines of Epekwitk. The first task in building an 18 to 24 foot canoe was to find a large birch tree that could provide the necessary bark. The frame or "ribs" of the canoe were made of cedar slats. The ribs were then covered in sheets of birch bark sewn together with fir roots. Birch bark canoes were waterproofed using fir gum chewed by women and children. Ocean-going Mi'kmaq canoes had elevated gunwales to prevent waves from splashing into the craft and were propelled using beech paddles. After Europeans arrived, sails were also used.

MI'KMAQ COMMUNITIES

The federal government recognizes two Mi'kmaq bands on PEI: the Abeqweit Band and the Lennox Island Band.

ABEGWEIT BAND

In all, the Abegweit band has a population of 318, of which 191 live on the three reserves of Morell, Rocky Point and Scotchford. Brian Francis was elected chief of the band in August 2007, and is aided by two councilors, Francis Jadis and Danny Levi.

JOHN JOE SARK:
GUARDIAN OF MI'KMAQ CULTURE

Mi'kmaq John Joe Sark has dedicated his life to his community and province. A 1985 graduate of the University of PEI, he has used his profound knowledge of his Mi'kmaq culture to press for Mi'kmaq social, political and cultural rights.

He has served as Band manager of his Lennox Island reserve, worked for fifteen years as a Community Resource Officer for the provincial government, and acted as curator of the Confederation Centre's Art Gallery. Sark has worked tirelessly to protect and strengthen his Mi'kmaq culture. One struggle saw Sark fight to have the name of a local school sports team changed. The Redmen, Sark argued, was an offensive name, made all the worse by team practices which mocked the culture and heritage of indigenous people. Ultimately, Sark's persistence paid off and the name was changed.

Sark has made his mark on the international stage. In 1993, he was appointed by the Mi'kmaq Grand Council to act as ambassador to the Vatican. Sark personally delivered a letter asking for the Roman Catholic church to apologize for its participation in Canada's legacy of residential schooling.

The following year he began a twelve year stint as ambassador to the United Nations Human Rights Commission in Geneva, during which time he helped draft the Declaration of Rights of Indigenous People. In 1999, he was named to the Acadian National Society in New Orleans and in 2002, to the Acadian National Society in France.

Sark has received many awards and accolades for his contributions. In 2005, he won the National Aboriginal Achievement Foundation's Award of Heritage and Spirituality. He has also been named a life Keptin of the Mi'kmaq Grand Council as keeper of spiritual and cultural integrity of the Mi'kmaq people.

LENNOX ISLAND BAND

The Lennox Island band has a total membership of 820, of which 380 live on the reserve. Darlene Bernard is Chief and is aided by councilors Robert Augustine, Donald Levi and Stephen Bernard.

POPULATION

- PEI has the smallest Aboriginal population in Canada. In contrast to Nunavut, where 85 percent of the population is Aboriginal, just 1.3 percent of PEI's population claims this ethnicity.
- Number of Aboriginal people on PEI: 1,730
- Number who claim Mi'kmaq as their mother tongue: 105
- Number who claim Inuktitut as their mother tongue: 15

Source: Statistics Canada.

UNEMPLOYMENT

In a province where the overall unemployment rate in 2014 rested at 12 percent, the problem of Aboriginal unemployment was even more acute. About one and a half times as many, 17.3 percent of Island Aboriginals were out of work that year.

Source: Statistics Canada.

THE FUTURE

While the median age for the whole province is 40.8, the median age of Aboriginals is 24.1.

Source: Statistics Canada.

Weblinks

Mi'kmaq Confederacy of PEI

www.mcpei.ca

This group was established in 2002 to create an Island society "that respects and sustains their existing aboriginal and treaty rights on PEI." Visit this site to read about the Confederacy, its programs and initiatives.

Mi'gmaq-Mi'kmaq Online Dictionary

www.mikmaqonline.org/

Check out this nifty online dictionary that contains more than 6,000 Mi'kmaq words. This website is for anyone interested in the fascinating Mi'kmaq language.

Go Ahead, Take Five More

As you can probably tell, we are partial to things you can count on one hand. This chapter is more of that, it is designed to be fun, but at the same time revealing, both about our province, and the person making the choices. It is a chapter that could have continued well beyond the bounds of this book. Islanders, famous and not so famous, were literally bursting at the seams with opinions about their province. This means, of course, we'll include more choices next time.

TAKE 5: STEVE KNECHTEL'S TOP FIVE BEST THINGS ABOUT THE CHARLOTTETOWN FARMERS' MARKET

For the past 25 years, Knechtel has made his living operating a bakery and flourmill. He produces a whole host of what are now called 'artisan' breads — products such as stone ground, wholegrain and sourdough bread. Knechtel has found a niche in the Island community, which is devoted to his product. The main outlet for his wares is the Charlottetown Farmers' Market, held year round on Saturday, 9am – 2pm, and in July and August, also on Wednesdays during the same hours. The Market is a 'must see' and is located at 100 Belvedere Ave.

1. **The Farmers' Market itself** has to be its best quality. When you have spent as many years there as I have, you come to love the place.

Given the wide range of people, customers and vendors who assemble there, and the wide range of food products, a day at the market is a moveable feast. Someone once said, "You can't live on bread alone" – obviously this person was not a baker. But without a doubt, you can live better than most on the fantastic selection of food products on tap at the Charlottetown Farmers' Market.

2. **The smell of fresh ground coffee** wafting from the Caledonia House booth. There is nothing like it first thing in the morning.

3. **The certified organic produce from Paul Offer's booth**. The Doctor's Inn grows amazing heritage tomatoes and, if you're lucky (and if you come early enough), you just might snaffle one of his giant peaches.

4. **Foxhollow Bakery's chocolate cake**. Need I say more? This definitely tastes like more.

5. **Johnny Flynn's Colville Bay oysters**. If you like oysters these are, in my humble opinion, the best on the Island. I should know – I sell them at my booth.

TAKE 5: KATHLEEN EATON'S FIVE PEI MUST READS

Kathleen Eaton is the chief librarian at Confederation Centre Public Library. It is the largest public library in Prince Edward Island and serves as the central library for the province. Located in downtown Charlottetown in the Confederation Centre of the Arts, the recently renovated facility is a vibrant community centre with 5,000 visitors each week enjoying library services, resources and programs.

1. *The Island Acadians, 1720-1980* by Georges Arsenault (1999)

TAKE 5: CHEF ANDREW MORRISON'S TOP FIVE THINGS TO EAT ON PEI . . . BESIDES LOBSTER!

As PEI's 2006 Chef of the Year and four time recipient of the CAA/AAA Four-Diamond Award for dining, Chef Andrew Morrison's philosophy on cooking is very simple: "If it's local . . . use it, if you don't know what to do with it . . . experiment." Chef Morrison is Chef at the famous Island resort, Dalvay by the Sea, a position he has held since 2003. Chef Morrison is a chef instructor at Holland College's Culinary Institute of Canada.

1. **Mussels:** They're found everywhere on PEI, are very inexpensive and are loaded with natural flavor. Steam them in wine and garlic or get a little fancier and try apples and cinnamon or fresh tomatoes and pesto. Island Gold is one of the larger producers of shellfish in Atlantic Canada —they strive to insure that the best and freshest mussels are available everywhere.

2. **Local produce:** It's hard to drive anywhere in the PEI countryside without passing a road-side stand displaying beautiful farm fresh fruit and vegetables. Local producers such as Countryside Produce, Alvin MacDonald and Jewell's have spent their lives perfecting their trade, and you will not find better produce anywhere in the world.

3. **Local beef:** The Island's first beef production plant, Atlantic Beef Products, produces quality beef comparable to (or better than) Western Black Angus. We are all about seafood here on the Island, but a little turf with your surf is never a bad thing!

4. **Oysters:** Malpeque oysters, considered the world's best, are found in many regions such as Malpeque Bay, Raspberry Point and Coville Bay. You can cook them if you wish, but there's nothing like eating them straight from the shell just minutes from being out of the water.

5. **Potatoes:** Irish Cobblers, Netted Jems, Russets, Yellow Fleshed, Fingerlings, Baby Reds, Baby Blues . . . I could go on. They are all local, all delicious and all very versatile. From mass production farms such as Lewis and Sons, to small producers of specialty potatoes such as Rare Earth Potato Company, potatoes are anything but plain around here. Cook off a few of your favorite potatoes, chill them and roughly dice them. Brown a little butter in a sauté pan, toss in the potatoes, season with salt and pepper and finish with sliced green onions, crumbled bacon, fresh baby spinach leaves and a couple of tablespoons of cream. Serve with any of your favorite seafood dishes. Even lobster.

TAKE 5: CHUCK & ALBERT'S TOP FIVE ACADIAN EVENTS ON PEI (IN NO PARTICULAR ORDER)

Chuck and Albert are no strangers to the art of total entertainment. Former members of the Acadian musical group Barachois, their performances bring to life the unique mixture of all-out sketch and caricature comedy routines and the upbeat foot stomping music of their indigenous PEI Acadian roots. To see the boys in action or to find out more, visit www.chuckandalbert.com.

1. L'Exposition Agricole et le Festival Acadien

A volunteer-run festival, it has been maintained in the Evangeline Area of PEI for over 100 years and is definitely a great place to get your fill of all things Acadian. Superb music, dancing, food, crafts, exhibits, heck there's even a cow-bingo! Don't miss the parade or the baptism of the boats.

2. Rendez-vous Rustico
Considered one of Canada's most unique and visionary songwriters, Lennie Gallant (or as we call him "Papa Cool") makes his yearly pilgrimage back home to headline his hometown's biggest party. A wonderful three-day family event showcasing this growing community's Acadian roots.

3. Souper-Spectacles (Translation : Dinner Theatres)
An even better translation — the best of both worlds! Take your pick during the summer months and enjoy a meal while sampling some of the local cuisine and talent at any of the following: La Cuisine À Mémé — located in Mont Carmel, V'nez Chou Nous — located in Tignish, or Le Centre Expo — located in Abram's Village.

4. Fête Roma
Located just north of Montague, this is a terrific event featuring music, entertainment, dance and food in 1700s style. Games, history lectures, a Latin Mass, a sumptuous Harvest Feast and over 50 re-enactors in 1700s style clothing help re-create the time of PEI's early French settlers.

5. The Acadian Museum
Here you can discover the odyssey of the PEI Acadians since 1720. An interpretive video, genealogy resources, a heritage trail, a gift shop and cool exhibits showcasing Acadian culture await your discovery. Though not an event per se, anything they have going on is worth the trip! It's definitely a good place to start.

TAKE 5: CHARLOTTETOWN'S MAYOR CLIFFORD LEE'S TOP FIVE BEST THINGS ABOUT HIS CITY

Mayor Clifford Lee is Mayor of the City of Charlottetown, capital city of Prince Edward Island. He was first elected to Charlottetown City Council as a Councillor in November of 1987 and served consecutive terms since then. In November of 2003 he was elected as Mayor and reelected again in November of 2006.

1. It's the birthplace of Confederation. In 1864, the first meeting to discuss the creation of Canada was held here.

2. In 2005 the City of Charlottetown celebrated its 150th Anniversary of Incorporation. We are a city proud of our heritage.

3. The architecture of the City.

4. Residents of Charlottetown genuinely care about each other and look out for each other.

5. Charlottetown has all the amenities of a larger city. It has, however, retained its uniqueness as a small relaxed city.

CHEF HANS ANDEREGG'S FIVE BEST RESTAURANTS IN PEI

Chef Hans Anderegg, 2009 National Chef of the Year and an instructor at Holland College's Culinary Institute of Canada, came to Canada from his native Switzerland more than 30 years ago. Over the years, he's seen a lot of restaurants come and go. Chef Hans compiled this list of his top five favourites, most of which are owned or run by graduates of The Culinary Institute of Canada.

1. The Lucy Maud Dining Room – The Culinary Institute of Canada, Charlottetown Waterfront.

The Lucy Maud Dining Room is situated overlooking the beautiful Charlottetown Harbour. Operated by the Culinary Institute of Canada, all meals are prepared and served by students of The Culinary Institute of Canada, and Tourism and Hospitality students and staff. The facility is open throughout the year, offering unique dining experiences. www.hollandcollege.com/lmdr

2. Lot 30

Located on Kent Street in the heart of downtown Charlottetown, Lot 30 is the pride and joy of Head chef and owner Gordan Bailey, and provides the highest level of service, the finest food, and the greatest atmosphere that Prince Edward Island has to offer. www.lot30restaurant.ca

3. Dalvay by the Sea

The dining experience at Dalvay, located about 20 minutes outside of Charlottetown on the north shore, has always been memorable for cuisine, ambiance and personal service. Under the direction of Chef Andrew Morrison, Dalvay maintains a tradition of offering the finest and freshest local ingredients. www.dalvaybythesea.com

4. The Pearl Café

The Pearl Café is an eclectic eatery located between the picturesque fishing village of North Rustico and Cavendish Beach tourist area. The café has been a Taste Our Island Award finalist in both of their first two years of operation. This award recognizes restaurateurs who support sustainable regional food systems. The menu changes often to reflect the seasonality of locally sourced ingredients. www.thepearlcafe.ca

5. Shipwright's Café

Located in Margate, Prince Edward Island, Shipwright's Café draws in locals and tourists from around the world. Chef Calvin Burt, with his love for local ingredients and culinary flair, has made Shipwright's Café a major destination on the Island culinary scene. www.shipwrightspei.com

TAKE 5: JACKIE WADDELL'S TOP FIVE REASONS TO PROTECT MORE NATURAL AREAS IN PRINCE EDWARD ISLAND

Jackie Waddell is the Executive Director of Island Nature Trust, a non-government, charitable organization devoted to the protection and management of natural areas on Prince Edward Island.

1. Permanently protected natural areas will provide sanctuaries for native plants and animals, if natural areas are protected in sufficient quantity and quality. Otherwise, the disappearance of species will continue at the current alarming rate.

2. Protected natural areas will produce clean air and protect clean water for all living things that need these precious resources.

3. Protected natural areas will produce future cures for disease, and currently provide many cures for what ails us, spiritually and physically. We had all better find out what is out there before it disappears, not after.

4. Protected natural areas are very few and far between and once adequate amounts are protected it will form a network of connected communities for the benefit of wildlife — human and otherwise.

5. More protected natural areas will provide more to the economy of the world than their destruction for human uses.

TAKE 5: JERRY MCCABE'S TOP FIVE HARNESS RACING DRIVERS FROM PEI

Jerry McCabe has a long association with PEI harness racing in various capacities as a judge, groom, fan and trivia master. He directed the research for the historical displays at the CDPEC. He is a member of the "Memory Lane" committee that helps preserve and display the Island's harness racing history and the Atlantic Breeders Crown Host Committee.

1. **Joe O'Brien** – Alberton-born Hall of Famer was one of the sports all-time greats.

2. **Wally Hennessey** – another member of the Hall of Fame, Wally has amassed over 6000 lifetime wins.

3. **Mark MacDonald** – set the Canadian record for most wins in a season in 2005 and again in 2006, while rising to the top of his sport.

4. **Paul MacKenzie** – with over 5500 lifetime wins, "Spook" has been a leading driver at Flamboro Downs in Ontario for nearly 20 years.

5. **Clark Smith** – still active as a trainer, "Clarkie" was among the leading drivers in the Maritime region from the late 1950s to early 1980's.

TAKE 5: COREY SLUMKOSKI'S TOP FIVE GO-KART TRACKS ON PEI

PEI enthusiast Corey Slumkoski has three favourite things to do on the Island. They are relaxing at the family's Canoe Cove cottage, eating barbeque and racing go-karts, preferably in that order! When he feels the need, the need for speed, these are the places he heads to.

1. Bonshaw 500 Go Kart Raceway

The karts may be old and the track may be simple, but this is the place we consistently return to, simply because all the go karts are quick and the track operators seem to recognize that "rubbin's racin'!"

2. Burlington Amusement Park and Go Karts

With faster karts and a longer track than Bonshaw, Burlington has a legit-imate claim to the title of Island's Best. You have to travel as far east as Montreal to find a longer track, and the presence of Kiddie Karts ensures that a new generation of Islanders will know the fun that is go-karting.

3. **Bridgeview Go Karts**

Located right at the end of the Confederation Bridge (or the beginning if you're leaving the Island), the Bridgeview track provides a wonderful way to begin (or end) your stay on the Island.

4. **Sandspit**

No trip to Cavendish is complete without a tour around Sandspit's figure eight track. Sadly, the popularity of Sandspit with families mean the karts tend to be on the slow side.

5. **Island Market Mini Golf**

If you're hitting the outlet shops at the North River Causeway just outside of Charlottetown, you owe it to yourself to check out the Island Market Mini Golf's go-kart track. Just be sure to watch a race or two, because at Island Market you can be sure one car is a lot faster than the others.